The Explorations of the La Vérendryes in the Northern Plains, 1738–43

G. Hubert Smith, a historian and an archeologist, retranslated the journals and reassessed the existing scholarship on the La Vérendrye expeditions in the 1950s. Mr. Smith was associated during the 1930s and 1940s with the Minnesota Historical Society, and in the 1950s and 1960s with the Smithsonian Institution's River Basin Surveys. Among his many historical studies are *Archeological Investigations at the Site of Fort Stevenson, North Dakota* (1960) and *Like-a-Fishhook Village and Fort Berthold, North Dakota* (1972). His La Vérendrye research, which has not previously been generally available, has been updated by W. Raymond Wood, a professor of anthropology at the University of Missouri–Columbia. Dr. Wood is the author of many publications on Northern Plains Indians and archeology, including *An Interpretation of Mandan Culture History* (1967), and is co-editor, with Margot Liberty, of *Anthropology on the Great Plains* (1980), also published by the UNP.

G. HUBERT SMITH

THE
EXPLORATIONS
OF THE
LA VÉRENDRYES
IN THE
NORTHERN PLAINS,
1738–43

Edited by W. Raymond Wood

UNIVERSITY OF NEBRASKA PRESS
LINCOLN AND LONDON

Library of Congress Cataloging in Publication Data

Smith, G. Hubert
  The explorations of the La Vérendryes in the
Northern Plains, 1738-43.

  Bibliography: p. 145.
  Includes index.
  1. La Vérendrye, Pierre Gaultier de Varennes, sieur de, 1685-1749. 2. La Véren-
drye family. 3. Northwest, Canadian—Discovery and exploration. 4. North Dakota—
History. 5. Explorers—France—Biography. 6. Explorers—Canada—Biography.
I. Wood, W. Raymond. II. Title.
F1060.7.L392S64   917'.04'3   79-26518
ISBN 0-8032-4712-5

Contents

Figures

Editor's Preface

THE first Europeans to enter the northern plains, and to leave a record of their passage, were members of the La Vérendrye family in the early decades of the 1700s. Although their records leave a great deal to be desired in terms of precise reference, they nevertheless are invaluable sources for the early historical period in what is now the north-central United States. No documents of comparable breadth for the area were to appear for more than sixty years, with the passage of the Lewis and Clark expedition. In this sense, the La Vérendrye documents rank with those describing the Spanish *entrada* into the central plains by Coronado, and into the American Southeast by De Soto and La Salle. Yet, for reasons that are not entirely clear, the accomplishments of the La Vérendrye family have not attained the prominence due them—in spite of the fact that most of the documents relating to their exploits have been available since the publication of Lawrence J. Burpee's edition of them in 1927.

Pierre Gaultier de Varennes, the Sieur de la Vérendrye, and his sons were the first to explore what is now western North and South Dakota, very possibly reaching as far west in their travels as the Big Horn Mountains of northeastern Wyoming. The importance of their explorations to present-day scholars, as well as to general readers, is manifest, for their records are the first to document that area and its native American occupants, including the Mandans, that tribe which was to become such a magnet for later traders and explorers in the northern plains.

The late G. Hubert Smith's study of the travels of the La Vérendryes is a notable scholarly achievement and an important contribution to the field of history dealing with the exploration of New France in the eighteenth century. I am deeply indebted to my colleague Thomas D. Thiessen for his permission to include in this preface the extensive data he collected on the La Vérendrye manuscript that Smith prepared, and for his support throughout the preparation of its revision for publication. Smith's manuscript has passed largely unnoticed since its completion in 1951, largely because of transient administrative matters relating to Vérendrye National Monument, a former unit of the National Park System in North Dakota. Smith's research was commissioned by the National Park Service to assess the historical authenticity of that monument as a locality actually visited by the La Vérendrye parties. His conclusions provided the impetus for the abolition of the monument as a historical area administered by the federal government. To view Smith's study in its proper perspective, it is necessary to review the circumstances concerning the creation and fate of Vérendrye National Monument.

Vérendrye National Monument consisted of 253.04 acres of land near the former town of Sanish in Mountrail County, North Dakota, set aside by presidential proclamation on June 29, 1917. Orin G. Libby, then secretary of the State Historical Society of North Dakota, had strongly advocated the reservation and administration of the area as a historical site under the aegis of either the state of North Dakota or the federal government.[1] Primarily at his instigation, the area was proclaimed a national monument. It was under the supervision of the superintendent of Wind Cave National Park and, later, of Theodore Roosevelt National Memorial Park; a resident of the town of Sanish was appointed custodian of the park. The single noteworthy feature within the park was Crow-Flies-High Butte (also known as Crowhigh Butte or Mountain), a 250-foot-high eminence upon which was set a granite boulder bearing a bronze plaque commemorating the presumed visits of the La Vérendryes to the locale.

A historian by formal training, Libby was the primary proponent of the idea that the two La Vérendrye expeditions had actually visited the Hidatsa Indians, rather than the Mandans as is commonly believed. He further maintained that the Hidatsas were at that time settled on the Missouri River a considerable distance above the Mandans, in the immediate vicinity of the mouth of the Little Knife River near the former town of Sanish (which has since been relocated and renamed New Town). This contention was not accepted by all authorities, and Smith's study is an effective rebuttal of Libby's arguments. A number of historians, from Francis Parkman in the 1890s to Russell Reid, a contemporary of Smith's, have attempted to delineate the routes traveled by the La Vérendryes in the northern plains of the present United States, but until Smith's work no comprehensive, in-depth review of the evidence was available from which to frame conclusions.

Although doubt existed as to the historical basis for Vérendrye National Monument, the impetus for Smith's research was actually provided by the planning for Garrison Dam, a large earthen dam across the Missouri River built in the late 1940s and early 1950s by the U.S. Army Corps of Engineers. When completed, the dam would back water up the Missouri valley for over a hundred miles and would result in the flooding of part of the monument lands.

Research to resolve the authenticity of the monument's location was undertaken by Olaf T. Hagen, regional historian in the Region Two office of the National Park Service in Omaha, but the effort ended in 1949 with Hagen's death. Consequently, the regional director of Region Two approached Dr. Grace Lee Nute of the Minnesota Historical Society, a noted fur trade historian, with a proposal for a comprehensive review of all available evidence pertaining to the explorations of the La Vérendryes in the northern plains. Dr. Nute recommended G. Hubert Smith, an anthropologist recently employed by the Minnesota Historical Society, for the task, and in July 1950 the National Park Service entered into a contract with Smith for an exhaustive critical review of the subject.

The contract provided $3,075 for the research, which was to be conducted over a period of nine months, from July 1950 through March 1951. Throughout the study, Smith maintained close coordination with the newly appointed regional historian for Region Two, Merrill J. Mattes, and obtained the assistance of several other eminent authorities on fur trade matters, including Grace Lee Nute, Abraham P. Nasatir, and W. Kaye Lamb. Smith consulted materials in the collections of the State Historical Society of North Dakota, the Minnesota Historical Society, and both the French and United States national archives, among others; and his research led him to visit Montreal, Three Rivers, and Quebec, as well as the several locales in the northern plains reputed to have been visited by the La Vérendryes.

Smith's report, completed in April 1951, conclusively refuted several earlier assertions about the La Vérendryes, including Libby's idea that the La Vérendrye parties had visited the vicinity of Vérendrye National Monument. He also made a number of recommendations regarding the administration of the monument, among which was one that the park not be disestablished because of historical inaccuracy, but rather that the monument be retained to commemorate the accomplishments of the La Vérendryes, so long neglected. These recommendations were forwarded to the director of the National Park Service by the regional director in June 1951, along with the original typescript copy of Smith's report.

The manuscript was reviewed at both the Washington and regional levels of the National Park Service, and, in consequence of Smith's arguments, the decision was made to recommend legislation to disestablish Vérendrye National Monument as a unit of the National Park system. In 1954, Russell Reid, on behalf of the State Historical Society of North Dakota, expressed an interest in acquiring the monument lands for use as a historic site under the administration of the society. Subsequently, in 1955 a bill sponsored by North Dakota representative Usher L. Burdick was introduced into the House of Representatives which would abolish the area's status as a national monument and authorize the conveyance of the land to the state of North Dakota for use as a historic site and recreation area. The bill also reserved the right of the United States to flood the park lands as a result of the filling of Garrison Reservoir, now known as Lake Sakakawea. On July 30, 1956, the bill was approved by Congress and Vérendrye National

Monument was stricken from the roster of national parks.[2] Today part of the former monument land lies beneath the waters of Lake Sakakawea.

It is ironic that G. Hubert Smith's research was used in support of the disestablishment of a park commemorating the achievements of a family in whom he maintained an interest throughout so much of his long and productive professional career. On August 6, 1956, Smith wrote a letter to the regional director of Region Two to register his embarrassment "over having been mentioned as having found evidence to support the disestablishment of the former monument, since the decision of the Service, however necessary, conflicts directly with my recommendations." Nevertheless, the overriding value of Smith's work lies in his scholarly contribution to knowledge of early European exploration in the Plains, not with the ephemeral consequences of his research.[3] And surely no contemporary scholar was more intimately familiar with the history of the area involved or better qualified to produce the document here published.

It is necessary to comment briefly on how Smith's manuscript was prepared for publication, as a prelude to several comments on the author himself. I have made a number of changes in the manuscript at the urging of an anonymous historian referee of the original draft and other changes in the light of comments by referees of the revised work. I am grateful to C. L. Dill, Elizabeth P. Henning, E. Leigh Syms, and Alan R. Woolworth for their constructive advice and criticism, which materially aided me in updating and revising the manuscript.

Among other things, I have removed an appendix that reviewed Smith's arguments against the authenticity of the location of the former Verendrye National Monument near Sanish (now New Town), North Dakota. This appendix simply summarized all of the points previously covered in the body of the report, so it provided no new material.

Second, because his manuscript was written for his peers in the National Park Service, it was more verbose and pedantic than one would expect a book for the nonspecialist reader to be. Consequently, I have lightened his monographic style and deleted or abbreviated numerous redundancies, without altering the sense. Although more than a quarter of a century has elapsed since the manuscript was written, all of Smith's conclusions stand herein as he perceived them at the time. For the most part, I found it necessary only to update his references and add citations to publications that have appeared since 1951. In some cases, manuscripts he cited were later published, and a number of reports published after his death in 1972 have been added to bring the references up to date. I have also had the advantage of access to a copy of Smith's personal copy of his paper—a manuscript which reflected changes he made for several years following submission of the work to the National Park Service. I am indebted to Alan R. Woolworth and to the Minnesota Historical Society for this courtesy.

It is a tribute to Hubert Smith's scholarship and to his attention to detail—as well as to his meticulous respect for the method of historical criticism—that his work merits publication so long after its completion, especially in this time of avalanching historical and archaeological data.

Those of us who were fortunate enough to know Hubert Smith not only loved him, and learned much from him, but admired his Old World manners and scholarship, and his impeccable standards of workmanship. If there is any sphere in which we might fault him, it was his deeply rooted personal modesty—a modesty which, combined with his deep respect for historical accuracy and his conviction that truth is elusive, inhibited the publication of this volume during his lifetime, and thus denied us his insight for so long.

For those who may wish to consult the unedited manuscript, the original typescript of his work, entitled "Explorations of the La Vérendryes, 1738–1743, with Special Reference to Vérendrye National Monument" (dated April 1951), is in the office of the director of the National Park Service. Copies of it are on file at the Midwest Archeological Center, Lincoln, Nebraska; at the Theodore Roosevelt National Memorial Park, Medora, North Dakota; in the Division of Archives and Manuscripts, Minnesota Historical Society, St. Paul; and in the editor's files. The two maps (figures 1 and 10) were especially drafted for this book by P. R. Trevathon, of Jefferson City, Missouri.

W. RAYMOND WOOD

Author's Preface

ABOUT 1851, the newly appointed archivist of the French
Second Republic, Pierre Margry, rediscovered the forgotten
records of the La Vérendryes in Colonial Office collections—
papers that had miraculously escaped the fires of the first
Bastille Day and the countless other hazards to which such
records are subject. He published them at once, in 1852, in the
new semiofficial Paris daily, the *Moniteur Universel.* In this
way they became known to Francis Parkman in Boston
(perhaps copies were sent to him by Margry), and when in 1888
he came to publish his own masterly account of this part of the
story of the French regime in the New World, Parkman gladly
acknowledged his debt to Margry, with whom he had long
corresponded, as the source of his knowledge of La Vérendrye.
Other students also seem to have known of Margry's discoveries
in the history of New France; thus George Catlin, in the first
pages of his book *O-kee-pa,* published in 1867, mentions the
"Brothers Verendrye" and their accomplishments, perhaps
having his information from the same published source. Pierre
Margry, himself, had been much interested in Catlin's efforts to
record the appearance of the American Indians in regions long
familiar to French colonials.

The La Vérendryes seem to have been neglected by the

earlier historians of the colony in Canada, though the family was descended from the first historian of New France, Pierre Boucher himself. Other authors writing from Canada, like Boucher, who unquestionably knew about the remarkable achievements of their compatriots from Three Rivers, make little mention of them. That the accomplishments of the family were never entirely forgotten is clear from a reference in about 1816, published in a series of articles by "Mercator," and appearing in the *Montreal Gazette*, concerned with the conflicting claims of the Northwest and Hudson's Bay companies. Still more time was to elapse before the work of the La Vérendryes—accomplishments that were not at the time known to the learned world, except in bits and pieces—could be seen in proper perspective.

A word is in order here justifying the detailed annotation and analysis offered in this book. The facts gathered by others, with their opinions, have been closely reexamined because many of the earlier investigations were careless and slipshod— indeed, beginning with Pierre Margry himself. All too often, acceptable critical standards were violated. The writing of history has of course changed radically in the century since Margry's first newspaper articles of 1852. It is therefore proper to point out recognizable errors of fact, and of judgment, with which the subject has become encumbered.

To allude to the shortcomings of previous scholars is far from disparaging their solid results, and the present-day student is heavily indebted to Pierre Margry, as well as to Francis Parkman, Lawrence Burpee, Orin G. Libby, Doane Robinson, George F. Will, and many others. As to Margry, whose hands were sometimes soiled in other historical ventures, it should be noted that there is no hint of any willful misrepresentation on his part in connection with the La Vérendryes.

G. HUBERT SMITH

Acknowledgments

Dur
ing the preparation of this study I have had the help of numerous persons, including Dr. Grace Lee Nute, Minnesota Historical Society; Dr. George F. Will and Mr. Russell Reid, State Historical Society of North Dakota; Dr. Abraham P. Nasatir, San Diego State Teachers College; the staff of the Missouri River Basin Surveys, Smithsonian Institution; and the staff of the Regional Office, Region Two (now the Midwest Region), National Park Service. The interest of these and numerous other persons is most gratefully acknowledged. I especially acknowledge the interest and assistance of Dr. W. Kaye Lamb, Dominion Archivist, and the staff of the Public Archives of Canada, and Dr. Nasatir's courtesy in loaning galley proofs of the introduction to his important study *Before Lewis and Clark.*

G. Hubert Smith

*The Explorations of the La Vérendryes
in the Northern Plains, 1738–43*

1
The Fur Trade and the Search for a Sea of the West

THE fur trade may be the most important single topic in the early history of much of Canada and the United States. For more than two centuries, in a vast part of North America, the history of this commerce is the framework upon which other historical themes must be spread; indeed, even discovery and exploration were, in large part, aspects of the fur trade.

The early eighteenth century was a time of wide and rapid territorial expansion in New France, under determined, capable leadership, and with constant reference to the fur trade. Among the men who figured in this expansion, the greatest was Pierre Gaultier de Varennes, the Sieur de la Vérendrye. A fur trader above all, La Vérendrye was given authority in 1727 to establish the Posts of the North, a string of small forts stretching westward from Lake Superior that challenged the English fur traders centered at Hudson Bay and established the claim of New France to the western country. Equally important, they were bases of further exploration of the interior of North America. In 1738 La Vérendrye, and in 1743 two of his sons, launched from these outposts of New France journeys of exploration far to the south and west.

In 1738, La Vérendrye went as far as the Missouri River; five years later, his sons approached some high, wooded

1

mountains, most likely the Big Horn Mountains in what is now northern Wyoming. More cautious interpretations of their journeys suggest they went no farther than the Black Hills. Where exactly the La Vérendryes went, and what they saw, and precisely what Indians they met on these expeditions have been subject to dispute. Although sympathetic attention has been given the La Vérendryes by a host of historians since the days of Margry and Francis Parkman, many misunderstandings—not to mention several serious errors—have become embedded in even the best accounts of their travels. This volume, in the light of new evidence, is focused especially on personal, local, and specific events of the years 1738–43, when the family penetrated to the Missouri River and beyond.

The boundaries of New France were never precisely determined, but the area included much of what has become Canada as well as the United States, for the two major divisions of New France were Canada and Louisiana. Much of the latter was later purchased for the United States by Thomas Jefferson in the Louisiana Purchase.

The fur trade of New France expanded rapidly westward from the St. Lawrence valley after the beginning of the eighteenth century, primarily under the necessity for opening new regions capable of producing furs, as Arthur S. Morton has noted.[1] Old hunting grounds in the drainage of the St. Lawrence River and along the lower Great Lakes were depleted after having been exploited for so long. At the same time, the French were feeling increasing competition from the English, through the Hudson's Bay Company. Furthermore, international wars at the turn of the century had seriously interrupted expansion of the fur trade in New France, upon which the very survival of the colony depended. With the Treaty of Utrecht, in 1713, the colony was once more able to pursue the fur trade without interruption. The provisions of the treaty were nevertheless severe for France, the loser in the War of the Spanish Succession, for the English had regained control of Hudson Bay, which had temporarily been given over in the course of the wars.

Caught between the English on the north and the Spanish

to the south and west, New France found it necessary to expand in a transcontinental, generally westward direction. It was at this time that La Vérendrye appears, in 1727, as commandant of the Posts of the North, probably the first director of this new administrative division of the ill-known inland hinterland of the settlements along the St. Lawrence valley.

New France was fortunate in having as governor general at this time Charles de la Boische, the Marquis de Beauharnois, who guided her development with honesty and ability for two decades after 1726. His own previous career had been largely in the military, which explains in part the military organization of such regions as the Posts of the North, although throughout its history the fur trade was often vested in military terms. The governor was fully aware of the urgent need for measures to combat foreign competition in the fur trade, as is clear from his remark that "if the savages find the French on their passage, they will not go in search of the English"—that is, they would not go to Hudson Bay.[2]

New France sent its explorers westward to search not only for new sources of furs, but also for a "Sea of the West" which would provide passage to the Indies.[3] The search was a manifestation of a renewed scientific interest in the natural world, but it was much more than that. As with the parallel search for a "Northwest Passage" by the English, the search for this western sea had obvious political and economic implications. The quest appealed strongly to the cultured French, fond of the arts and learning, and her court saw in a successful quest added prestige for the throne of the Bourbons, as well as a more favorable balance of world power.

Even before the beginning of the eighteenth century, in large part as a result of previous achievements of French colonials themselves, the attention of the court at Versailles and of colonial administrators at Quebec had concentrated on this goal, far beyond the well-known Great Lakes.[4] Although the French speculated on the character of the area to be crossed, they could scarcely have comprehended the vast distances involved. It is also understandable that the search was based on the hope of a water passage to the East: after all, all previous experience in New France had shown it to be a land of lakes and streams, seemingly without end. Exploration had proceeded with ever accelerating speed on these primitive highways.

The French and French colonials seem not to have fully realized that they knew but a small part of the whole; the real nature of the continent beyond the northeastern land of woods and waters had not yet been discovered. How could they have guessed that beyond this region were vast prairies and plains— vaster even than their familiar woodlands—and beyond them, the great Rocky Mountains, extending from arctic to tropic? Even informed geographers were ignorant of the character of this part of the continent, and as late as 1752, Joseph N. Delisle, one of the ablest and best informed of European cartographers, still showed the goal on one of his maps, a Mer de l'Ouest.[5] Early in the eighteenth century there were many accounts, both real and fictitious, of voyages of discovery on the Pacific Ocean. Such accounts were influential in reviving and stimulating an interest in the Sea of the West—an interest that probably never really disappeared, although it often became dormant.

The speculations of one Father Bobé, an obscure cleric in Paris, exemplify the interest that many people had in this subject just before the western explorations of LaVérendrye and his group.[6] Bobé's choice of routes for the search was the waterway west from Lake Superior, though he considered other possibilities. This route was already known in part to adventurous independent traders in New France. One such pioneer was Jacques de Noyon, who had gone trading, probably in 1688, as far west of Lake Superior as Rainy Lake, and had gained some knowledge of the region beyond as far as Lake of the Woods. Even farther west, he had been told, was a "western sea"—probably Lake Winnipeg.

In 1716, officials of New France urged that formal explorations be undertaken in this direction, and referred to the knowledge gained by de Noyon. It is clear that they were concerned about the commerce of New France, for they proposed the establishment of trading posts to intercept the Indian trade that was going to the English on Hudson Bay. After these posts were established, they suggested, a small expedition could be sent to the Western Sea. Their proposals found royal favor and were approved to the extent that a decree was even issued that the necessary expenses should be borne by the king. The result was the establishment, the following year, of the first such western post, at Kamanistikwia, by Zacherie Robutel, the Sieur de la Noue, and an expedition as far as the land of the Sioux to obtain peace between them and the tribes of the forest regions. Officials of the Hudson's Bay Company at York Fort became aware at once of the French penetration. "Under the thin veil of the Search for the Western Sea," as Morton put it, the French were aggressively pushing the trade into the border lake region in what is now Minnesota, Ontario, and Manitoba.[7]

Keen interest at court in exploration led to the dispatch to Canada of the Jesuit scholar Father Pierre-François-Xavier Charlevois to make personal inquiries concerning the best means of searching for a Western Sea and to undertake a preliminary reconnaissance himself. He spent the years 1720 and 1721 in "interviews and inquiries" and in traveling by way of the Lakes and the Mississippi River to its mouth. In his reports, submitted in 1723, he urged explorations up the Mississippi or Missouri rivers, and, faithful to his vows, he advised the establishment of a mission among the Sioux, where, he suggested, missionaries could gather information on the matter of the search for the Western Sea.[8]

As Charlevoix had recommended, Jesuit missionaries were assigned to duty among the Sioux. Although further exploration was not undertaken at the time, a fort was established in 1727 by Réné Boucher, the Sieur de la Perrière, among the Sioux on Lake Pepin, on the upper Mississippi River. It was christened Fort Beauharnois, and its spiritual advisers were the Fathers Michel Guignas and Nicolas de Gonor. The post was established by a company licensed by the governor, and Beauharnois himself was its most prominent shareholder. Another purpose of the venture is also revealed by the governor's statement that this post was needed to ensure the success of La Vérendrye's undertaking, he having just been appointed commandant of the Posts of the North. It was essential that the Sioux be friendly, Beauharnois wrote, "to allow of our trading with the Assiniboin and Cree, through whose country one must pass to the discovery of the Western Sea."[9]

The search for a Western Sea held a special appeal for the Jesuits, patrons of learning who were ever seeking new mission fields, as well as for the court, "whose desire for fresh geographical knowledge was an adornment to their characters and an honour to their time." The point of view in New France was, however, somewhat different; the search, with its ever receding goal, "never failed to minister to the expansion of the colony and to bring about a recovery of its fur trade when the beaver areas were depleted."[10] The search was therefore made to serve the economic needs of the colony.

It was the policy of the colonial administrators to encourage interest in the Sea of the West, "but always on the assumption that forts for fur trade would be established and the exploration as such relegated to some more convenient season." If that season never came, "no great harm would be done, for French arms would have been carried far afield and the stream of French furs would continue to flow through full banks." Such was the official policy at Quebec before La Vérendrye's time, and it helps explain his enterprise and the unfailing support he received from the governor and intendant at Quebec, as Morton has pointed out. When La Vérendrye proposed to open these western fur fields, already known to be rich, his proposal very naturally won official support in New France. An added inducement—one calculated to win the support of the court and of influential Jesuits—was that such expansion "offered some promise, however distant, of an easy route by canoe to the long-dreamed-of Sea of the West, wherever that might be."[11]

Something must now be said of the native peoples living near the Posts of the North, among whom La Vérendrye and his group were to spend so many years. Two such groups, especially important because of the role they were to play in French expansion westward from Lake Superior, were the Assiniboins and the Crees. Related to the Crees, in some now obscure manner, were the Monsonis, a smaller group. Not only were these tribes consumers of goods and producers of pelts, but they played the very important part of middlemen, trading goods obtained from the French for furs they obtained from more distant tribes, as well as their own furs, and providing pelts to the French in greater quantities than would otherwise have been possible.

The Crees and Monsonis were members of that vast group of Indians who spoke dialects of Algonquian, a language stock named from that of the first native groups met by explorers along the lower St. Lawrence. Among other members of this large language family were many tribes prominent in the history of New France: the Ottawas, like the Crees long famous as middlemen in the fur trade; the Chippewas, sometimes known as the Saulteurs; the Sauks and Foxes; and many others.

The livelihood of the native tribes in central Canada was derived chiefly from hunting and fishing. The migratory nature of the game upon which they depended, together with seasonal fishing, explains much of their nomadism. The balance between climate, topography, and the food supply was always a precarious one. The great physiographic area north of the Great Lakes—the Laurentian Shield—is dominated by woodlands, becoming generally poorer and less hospitable as one moves toward the north. The area is nevertheless one of abundant fur-bearing animals, and it was destined to be heavily exploited by both French and English fur traders.

The Crees once inhabited a vast area, ranging from the western shores of James Bay (the southernmost extension of Hudson Bay) to the southwest, past Lake Nipigon, through the border lakes country, and toward Lake Winnipeg. Their movements and lifeways were closely adjusted to a variable and migratory food supply. The surviving records of these peoples during the early contact period are scanty and often con-tradictory and confusing.

Even the very divisions of the Crees are in doubt. At an early date the Jesuits recorded that the Crees consisted of four major divisions. Of these, the group living about Lake Nipigon is mentioned first, and was doubtless that part of the Crees that is best known. During the nineteenth century there appear to have been two major divisions of this tribe: the Plains Crees and the Woods Crees, and the group is so described by anthropologists today.[12]

The early history of the Assiniboins is little better understood than that of the Crees, for again we lack adequate early documents. Native tradition is authority for the belief that the Assiniboins split off from another group (probably the Yanktonai Sioux), perhaps about 1640, just before the Assiniboins became known to the French. The area occupied by this group at the beginning of the historical period was south of Cree territory. The Assiniboins were the most northern branch of the great Siouan language stock, which centered about the Eastern Sioux (usually referred to as the Santee Sioux), then occupying the region of Mille Lacs Lake, in what is now Minnesota. This language stock included such other groups as the Yankton, Yanktonai, and Teton Sioux, as well as more distantly related groups such as the Omahas and Iowas. The Mandans and Hidatsas were also Siouan-speaking tribes. The remarkable earth lodge culture of these latter two tribes of the upper Missouri River will be given special attention in later pages.

The western explorations of the La Vérendryes, especially their travels in the 1738–43 period southwest of the present-day city of Winnipeg, Manitoba, were not isolated events in the history of New France. Rather, these journeys were final acts in a play begun at least a century before, in explorations westward from the then tiny settlements on the St. Lawrence. They were, moreover, related to other contemporary efforts (both official and unauthorized) on the part of French colonials from New Orleans, the other center of French settlement in the New World. This fact seems to have been overlooked by some scholars, intent upon the achievements of the La Vérendryes. Some students of La Vérendrye, indeed, seem to have been quite unaware of the fact that a great deal had already been accomplished in the exploration of the Missouri River basin from

New Orleans, and that La Vérendrye in 1738 and 1739 missed meeting—by only a few months—other French traders and explorers who had gone by way of the Missouri and its tributaries as far north as present South Dakota, at the same time he had reached the region by pushing westward from Lake Superior.[13]

The first important effort to trace the course of the Missouri River toward its sources appears to have been that of Etienne Veniard, the Sieur de Bourgmont. Details of his life are obscure, but enough has been preserved to justify the epithet of *adventurer*.[14] Having deserted his command at Detroit, Bourgmont fled sometime after 1707 to Louisiana, where he lived among the Indians of the lower Missouri for at least a decade. During that time he seems to have wandered far, though the regions he visited are uncertain. In about 1717, however, he composed a memoir describing the course of the Missouri as far upstream as the villages of the Arikaras, who were the downstream neighbors of the Mandans and Hidatsas. The Arikaras were members of yet another major language stock, Caddoan, to which the Pawnees also belonged. From the evidence of another document prepared by Bourgmont, dated 1714, it appears that most of his travels were made in that year, and the document provides his itinerary.[15]

Various memoirs from Louisiana for the years 1716–19 sought to draw the attention of the colonial ministry to the Missouri River as a route to new Mexico, long a matter of special concern in Louisiana.[16] In 1719 the Missouri and Osage rivers were ascended by an official expedition under the command of Charles-Claude du Tisné which met the Osage and Pawnee Indians and obtained information concerning the Padoucas (Comanches).[17] Now Bourgmont appeared once more, as a commandant of the Missouri region, and in 1723 he established a post on the north bank of the Missouri River in what is now Carroll County, central Missouri, which was named Fort d'Orléans. From this fort Bourgmont established relations with the Missouris, Kansas, Iowas, and other tribes. Although events of this period on the lower Missouri River do not concern us here, it is significant that as early as 1734 a fur trader among the Pani-mahas (the Skidi Pawnees, living in what is now eastern Nebraska) is mentioned by Bienville, the governor of Louisiana, as having visited the Arikaras.[18]

About 1739, commercial relations had been established between the French in Louisiana and the Spanish settlements in present-day New Mexico. At the same time, actual occupation of the Missouri valley had been pushed as far upstream as the present state of Kansas. Fort Cavagnolle was built near what is now Kansas City, and the same year the brothers Pierre and Paul Mallet succeeded in reaching Taos and Santa Fe. The Mallet brothers came into contact with some of the Arikaras at this time, as Bourgmont may also have done at an earlier date, but it is not certain that the Arikaras had as yet actually been visited in their own villages, which at this time were along the Missouri River in what is now central South Dakota.

The westward explorations of the La Vérendryes thus closely coincided with explorations from the south, both of which were reaching toward the northern plains and the upper Missouri River. In one instance the objective was the discovery of a Sea of the West, which should afford passage to the Far East; in the other, the objective was to establish routes from the Mississippi and Missouri rivers toward the settlements in New Spain. Each effort at penetration had a distinct commercial overtone, though of a somewhat different character. Each venture contributed, however, to the geographical knowledge of the realms of Louis XV of France.

2
History of the La Vérendryes
to 1738

FRENCH colonials had begun to acquire knowledge of the region beyond Lake Superior toward Lake Winnipeg well before the end of the seventeenth century. It was not, however, until the establishment of a new western command in 1727 that systematic and official exploration and occupation of the region began in earnest. This turning point in the affairs of New France was marked by the rise of La Vérendrye, who, with the assistance of his four sons, his nephew, and a group of business associates, capably managed the region for nearly twenty years. If in the end La Vérendrye found himself out of favor and financially ruined, there is no hint in the surviving sources that he was in any way incompetent; if he died in poverty, his failure was in large part a result of forces beyond his control. In any case, he must have felt pride in the knowledge that his efforts had carried far afield the flag of France, had served well the interests of the colony, and had greatly increased geographical knowledge.

Between Quebec, governmental center of New France, and Montreal, its commercial center, lay the village of Trois Rivières (Three Rivers), settled even before Montreal itself, probably in 1634. This settlement lay at the junction of two major fur routes, the St. Lawrence–Ottawa and the St. Maurice rivers, and became "a great nursery of valorous explorers and fur traders."[1] Among other well-remembered names from this village are those of Jean Nicolet, Médard Chouart Groseilliers, Pierre-Esprit Radisson, and Nicholas Perrot. But none is better remembered than that of Pierre Gaultier de Varennes, the Sieur de la Vérendrye. Even today at Three Rivers a civic monument to the memory of such men carries, beneath a fanciful bust of La Vérendrye, the legend "The most illustrious of the trifluviens." High praise has also been paid him by more sober historians. Harold A. Innis, in fact, remarks that La Vérendrye achieved no less than establishing the present boundary of Canada.[2]

Pierre Gaultier, the fourth son of René Gaultier de Varennes, governor of Three Rivers, was born there on November 17, 1685. The original record of his birth is still preserved in the parish register.[3] Little is known of his early years, but it cannot be doubted that he was nourished on the fur trade, in which his father was active. He must have heard— often at first hand from such venturesome members of the community as Jacques de Noyon and Nicholas Perrot—much of the lore of the western waters that he himself was to make known to the world.

La Vérendrye's ambitions seem to have first been fixed on a military career, and he entered the army (as was then possible) at the age of twelve. After serving in raids on the borders of New England and in Newfoundland, he took part in the campaigns in Flanders. Years later he compiled his own service record, from which we know he was severely wounded in 1709 at the Battle of Malplaquet, one of the last engagements between French and English forces in the War of the Spanish Succession, and was a prisoner for fifteen months.[4]

A reduction of the army with the impending treaty of peace probably left little hope of promotion for a colonial officer "of limited means and influence," and he returned to his home in 1711. Even before his service in Flanders he had, in the formal old French fashion, contracted to marry Marie-Ann du Sable, daughter of Louis Dandonneau du Sable, the Sieur de l'Ile du Pas.[5] If he was but a colonial, without interest or favor in the mother country, the future explorer in Three Rivers had the best connections.

Little is known of his life immediately following his return from the wars except that he had a trading post on the St. Maurice River called La Gabelle (The Excise Tax), the name of which was probably a thrust at governmental revenue-producing devices. The post was at a point "well calculated to catch the traffic with the Indians before it reached the town."[6] We may assume that the post was a profitable one, for at the time of his appointment to the Posts of the North, La Vérendrye seems to have had a great deal of influence well beyond Three Rivers.

His marriage, performed at Quebec in the fall of 1712, produced four sons and a daughter. These sons were to play a major part in the work of their father, and they were heirs of his ability.

The eldest son, Jean-Baptiste, born September 5, 1713, accompanied his father to the west as early as 1731, and himself established the first Fort Maurepas, on the Red River, three years later, a task assigned him by his father. Jean-Baptiste's skill in dealing with the Indians is evident during his short life, which ended on Lake of the Woods when he was only twenty-three. The hints we have of his personality suggest that he was fully at home among the Indians, perhaps more so than he would have been at his own birthplace.

The second son, born December 26, 1714, and named Pierre after his father, was a steady, reliable assistant. Like his older brother, Pierre was with his father in the west as early as 1731, and some ten years later himself founded Fort Dauphin, probably on Lake Manitoba. He seems to have been a good "right arm" for his father, whom he survived. The last glimpse we have of him is as an ensign of foot at Quebec, where he died in 1755.

The third son, François, born December 22, 1715, is of particular interest, for he was the Chevalier who, with the fourth and youngest son, in 1742 and 1743 visited the upper Missouri River, penetrating well beyond the river itself and their father's farthest reach.[7] François had joined his father in

1731 and accompanied him on his visit to the Missouri River in 1738. The next year he explored along the Saskatchewan River. After his father's death, François obtained a commission in the army and served in the final struggle in New France, in the Seven Years' War. Becoming a British subject, François lived unmarried at Montreal, and there he died in 1794, the last of the immediate family.

Louis-Joseph, born November 9, 1717, the youngest of the sons, joined his father in the trade in the West in 1735, having been specially trained in mathematics and drawing, and accompanied him to the Missouri River in 1738. After his subsequent journey west of the Missouri with François, Louis-Joseph also served in the army. In 1761, he was drowned in the wreck of the ship *Auguste*, which was carrying colonials returning to France.

Another member of La Vérendrye's staff was a nephew. His name, had he survived the hardships of the trader's life, might have been as well remembered as that of his uncle and his cousins. He was Christophe Dufrot, baptized December 7, 1708, the youngest son of Christophe Dufrot, the Sieur de la Jémeraye, and Marie-Renée Gaultier, the eldest sister of La Vérendrye. The nephew Christophe, best known as the Sieur de la Jémeraye, was in the west among the Sioux, Foxes, and Winnebagos as early as 1727, about the time of his uncle's first western venture.[8]

Sometime after 1727 La Jémeraye joined La Vérendrye, and upon his departure for the West in 1731 La Vérendrye took his nephew with him. Later in the year La Jémeraye was sent to establish Fort St. Pierre on Rainy Lake, the first of a chain of new posts built under La Vérendrye's direction. The nephew carried out still other orders with skill, and he must have been sorely missed after his early death, probably from disease or exposure, in 1736. La Jémeraye seems to have had more than ordinary ability, and probably more than ordinary training, since he prepared at least one well-drawn map of this part of the new regions, the original of which is still preserved.

Such was the composition of the immediate group La Vérendrye had with him in the West. Three Jesuits also accompanied him for shorter periods of time. These were Father Charles-Michel Mesaiger (1690–1766), who was present at the establishment of Fort St. Charles on Lake of the Woods in 1732, but who left the West the following year; Father Jean-Pierre Aulneau (1705–36), who was to die a violent death on Lake of the Woods with Jean-Baptiste de La Vérendrye and a group of canoemen; and Father Claude Godefroy Coquart (1706–65) who, recently arrived from France, in 1741 accompanied La Vérendrye as far as Michilimackinac. Later that year he apparently accompanied Pierre, the son, to Lake Manitoba.[9]

It is unfortunate that, except for a group of valuable personal letters of Father Aulneau, little has come down to us from the hands of these clerics.[10] The Jesuits were frequently able writers, and much that these priests recorded has probably been lost—material that would be of great value in tracing the accomplishments of La Vérendrye and his group. Something of this kind may have escaped the destruction of the archives of the order at Paris during its suppression, and more may be found in its archives in Rome. If this should prove to be the case, historians can look forward to fresh materials on subjects to which the Jesuits contributed so much—manners and customs of the Indians, geographical knowledge, and like matters. Such additions to knowledge for the upper Missouri region for this period, and upon which Coquart must have informed himself, would be especially welcome, since other sources on the explorations of the La Vérendryes are so tantalizingly brief.

When Pierre Gaultier, the Sieur de la Vérendrye, was appointed commandant of the Posts of the North in 1727, there were only three such posts: Kamanistikwia, Nipigon, and an outpost at Michipicoten. These posts had been stations by which the French had attempted to wrest the trade from the English in the valleys of the Moose and Albany rivers and in the Rainy Lake–Lake Winnipeg region to the west. Members of the Hudson's Bay Company became aware of the new pressure almost immediately. In 1728, its governor at Fort Albany asserted that the French—with the Assiniboins—yearly made war on most of the natives that frequented his post. He went on to add that the French had a settlement a mere four days'

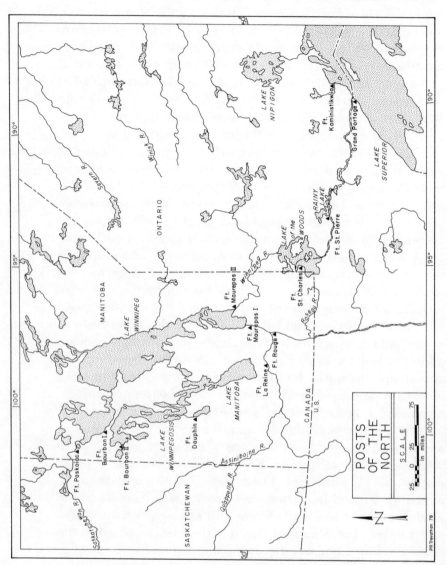

Fig. 1. La Vérendrye's Posts of the North, western New France.

paddling from Lake Winnipeg—probably evidence of the activities of nameless outrunners from La Vérendrye's post at Kamanistikwia.[11]

There is ample evidence that the French were quite familiar with the route to Lake Winnipeg well before the 1730s, and that they understood the relationship to Hudson Bay of this body of water. Pioneers had of course reached in this direction from the St. Lawrence at least forty years earlier. The profits of the trade in this quarter were considerable: one report asserted that the returns from the Posts of the North exceeded thirty thousand *livres* (perhaps six thousand dollars); that the officers there were concerned only with their own interests; and that, by rights, the profits of the trade should be reserved for the royal treasury. This report was scarcely an unbiased one, and its author was probably envious of the success of such persons as La Vérendrye and was transmitting to the ministry of colonies what it would certainly be pleased to hear. It doubtless did La Vérendrye harm and confirmed the Comte de Maurepas, the minister, in his opinion that this colonial officer "was nothing but a fur-trader seeking to amass a fortune."[12]

Whatever the intent of such reports, or their effects at court—and this was but one of many that seem to have reached it intended to discredit or reflect upon the motives of La Vérendrye—there is no evidence that the new governor, Beauharnois, was then or later influenced by them. Quite the opposite, for on May 19, 1731, La Vérendrye and a group of merchants contracted at Montreal to trade at the post of Ouinipigon, and their agreement was approved by the governor in the name of the king.[13] The region in which they were to trade, only vaguely defined in the minds of all concerned, was probably intended to include all of the vast area of the rivers draining to the west, at least as far as Lake Winnipeg. The contract is therefore a token of the esteem in which La Vérendrye was held in New France at this time by both merchants and officials. Almost at once La Vérendrye, La Jémeraye, and La Vérendrye's three eldest sons left for the West.

La Vérendrye had been in charge of the Posts of the North for only a short time before he began planning to push westward beyond the familiar regions around Lake Superior. It is quite probable that his command included a charge to explore the region, but of this there is no documentary evidence. In 1728, in any event, we know that La Vérendrye met Father Nicholas Gonor, returning from Fort Beauharnois, at Michilimackinac, and there they discussed the matter of exploration toward the west. Soon after, the priest wrote the governor, giving a summary of La Vérendrye's opinions on the problem.[14]

La Vérendrye had by this time gathered a good deal of information concerning the West from the natives who frequented his post at Kamanistikwia, and he submitted his report (probably compiled in 1729) to the governor personally in 1730.[15] From this document we have the first new bits of knowledge of the more distant West and of the peoples with whom La Vérendrye was to be so closely associated in the years to come.

The best informants were apparently the Crees of the area around Kamanistikwia. The extent of their travels (or of their claims of travel) is truly surprising, but there can be no doubt that they ranged great distances from their homes, following the border lakes west of Lake Superior, as well as moving in other directions. Pako, a chief in the Lake Nipigon region, and Le Foye (the Faithful One) and Petit Jour (Daybreak), his brother, said they had been west beyond a height of land, of which La Vérendrye was unaware, and had reached a great river flowing toward the setting sun—possibly the Winnipeg River. Their description of the country, its animals, and its native peoples and their statements provided the background for La Vérendrye's first real explorations in 1731. These peoples, they said, were very numerous and always wandering about, "never staying in any fixed place, but carrying their dwellings [cabannes] with them continually, from one place to another, and always camping together to form a village." These were the Assiniboins, long known to traders beyond Lake Superior as tipi-dwelling, bison-hunting nomads of the northern plains.

But the Crees of Kamanistikwia were also aware of more distant peoples, in part at least from actual travel to the west.

Their statements, preserved by La Vérendrye, are the earliest known reports of contacts from this quarter with peoples living along the Missouri River. Much of what the commandant of the Posts of the North was told of these distant tribes he was later to verify in person.

About three hundred leagues—nearly nine hundred miles—beyond the nomadic Assiniboins, the Crees asserted, were nations of a different character who lived in sedentary villages, raised crops, and "for lack of wood" made themselves huts of earth (*cahutes de terre*). As early as 1729, then, La Vérendrye had been reliably informed of the Missouri valley Indian groups, whose culture stood in sharp contrast to that of their nomadic neighbors to the north and east. His later personal visit to the homeland of these groups was thus but the culmination of an acquaintance of at least a decade. In fact, La Vérendrye and his sons actually met a few individuals from the Missouri valley villages before exploring in their direction, so were themselves aware of their different customs. Although the village tribes of the Missouri River had, beyond doubt, already traded with the English or with their middlemen, almost nothing was known of them before La Vérendrye's visit.

Other statements were made by the Crees about a river whose waters seemed as red as vermilion—surely the Red River of the North, which was to figure in La Vérendrye's explorations. They spoke also of less credible wonders, such as a small mountain whose stones sparkled "night and day," and which was called "The Dwelling of the Spirit" and no one ventured to approach. He was also told of a very fine gold-colored sand along the river of the "red waters." These tales were, of course, properly folklore, and have a certain authenticity as such. There are numerous hills to which the tales may have referred, which in native lore were the dwelling places of sacred beings. But the gold-colored sand—did the explorer hear aright, or did he imagine that in this region was some of the fabulous wealth that seems to attach itself to tales of distant lands?

In more credible realms, the Crees asserted that the Indians of the interior (*les Sauvages des terres*) had some knowledge of a river that flowed to the west. Some spoke of it from having seen it themselves, and others only from having been told of it, but all obligingly agreed in what they said of it. As proof of their reports, La Vérendrye recorded that in the fall of 1728, certain Crees had visited Kamistikwia, accompanied by people from those distant lands, permitting La Vérendrye actually to meet members of the village tribes of the Missouri River far from their homes.

One such person was a male slave mentioned in his account. This Indian, taken prisoner by the Assiniboins, had been given to a Cree chief. He had been captured along the River of the West, and himself gave additional details of the strange new peoples of those regions. The villages there were very numerous, he claimed, many of them being as much as two leagues long, and the country back from the river, as well as that fronting the river, was inhabited. The peoples there, he said, raised quantities of grain, fruits abounded, and game was plentiful. The inhabitants of these villages did not know what a canoe was, and since there was no wood in all this vast region, they used the dried dung of animals for fuel. In these statements we can see that authentic descriptive details of the Missouri River villagers were reaching La Vérendrye, mingled as they were with some statements difficult to understand, as well as some that need not be believed at all—such as that there was on the bank of the river a nation of dwarfs no more than three feet or so in height. Such lore of dwarfs in the Missouri basin was recorded also by later explorers, among them Lewis and Clark.

La Vérendrye's report of 1730 also contained such information as he could obtain concerning the actual routes by which one might reach the River of the West. Several crude maps were also made for him by Indians. Some asserted that white people lived at the mouth of the great western river, though they could not tell to what nation they belonged, for the length of the journey was such that none had ventured to make the trip. In order to do so, they said, it would be necessary to leave the Lake of the Woods in March and not hope to return before November. Such reports, La Vérendrye knew, were founded only on hearsay. Since the Crees could supply all their wants by trading with the English, only twenty days' travel distant, what would they be likely to seek on the Western Sea?

The Crees, he knew, were actually trading on Hudson Bay, and he remarked to Beauharnois: "The English have every interest in getting ahead of us, and if we allow them they will not lose the chance of doing it. Besides, the colony will receive a new benefit [from explorations to the west] independent of the discovery of the Western Sea, through the quantity of furs that will be produced and which go to waste among the Sioux and Assiniboin, or by way of the Cree go to the English."[16] La Vérendrye foresaw that no exploration could be accomplished apart from the trade and agreed with others in New France that the good of the colony would best be served by trade, whereas a search for a Sea of the West might be of little practical advantage.

Some days after receiving La Vérendrye's memoir, the governor forwarded it to the minister of colonies, together with a map prepared by a skilled engineer and draftsman of his circle at Quebec, the Sieur Chaussegros de Lery. This map was a compilation of the new information provided by native maps, together with information gathered by La Vérendrye, but reduced to a uniform scale and adjusted to one of the official maps of the royal geographer, Guillaume Delisle. The governor and his assistant agreed that the River of the West must flow into the Pacific Ocean, its mouth said to have been discovered the preceding century by the Spaniard Martín Aguilar. They also noted that there were two major rivers arising near the center of New France. One, flowing east, was of course the St. Lawrence; the other, flowing south, was the Mississippi. This arrangement, they argued, left a large territory to the west—in the region of the River of the West, of which much was now being heard. What is probably the original of the map prepared by de Lery has been preserved. Beauharnois's description of it, mentioning an attached sheet or slip of paper, leaves little doubt that in this case we have a particular map referred to in the documents of the period—something frequently difficult, if not impossible, to determine.[17]

Beauharnois and Giles Hocquart, the intendant, could readily see the logic of La Vérendrye's desire to extend the trade of the colony and his eagerness to enhance the prestige of New France through explorations, and did not hesitate to commend

him to Maurepas. But the minister had his doubts and submitted the various papers to Charlevoix for review. The Jesuit
surely sensed the mood of the minister, for he remarked that the
proposed exploration "might degenerate into a mere business of
fur trading," whereas the discovery of the Sea of the West was a
matter "which should be carried through continuously without
a stop." At the same time he observed, "After all, it is possible
that the Western Sea is so distant and the road thither so im-
practicable, that the discovery would be of no use to us."
Aware, however, of the minister's interest in exploration, he
shrewdly added, "On the other hand, it may also be com-
paratively near and easy to reach, and we have rivals whom we
ought to anticipate; and then, besides, in our search for it that
may happen . . . that in searching for what we are not destined
to find, we may find what we were not looking for and what
would be quite as advantageous to us as the object of our
search."[18] Surely not every benefit could be lost, whatever of
Charlevoix's counsel was to prevail!

Beauharnois had hoped that La Vérendrye's plea for
expenses for exploration would be approved by the king. But it
was the decision of the court that La Vérendrye should make
these efforts at his own expense. The colonials were of course
acting in their own best interests: for them the search for a
Western Sea would "expand the colony and rehabilitate the fur
trade which was, as it were, its life's blood. They aimed at the
occupation of the west to this end, and only envisioned exploration as to be carried out at some convenient time and at
the King's expense."[19] But La Vérendrye was already on his
way to the West when the decision was rendered, unaware of
the major change in his plans and intent on building posts as far
as Lake Winnipeg. In doing so he doubtless felt a certain
patriotism, for he would be, he wrote, "carrying the King's
arms far afield, enlarging the colony, and extending its commerce."[20]

The rightful claim of the La Vérendryes to the title *explorers* may be said to date from 1731, when, having contracted with certain merchants to supply the necessary goods
for trading, La Vérendrye, La Jémeraye, and three of La

Vérendrye's sons departed for the West with the approval of the governor, and acting for the king. Now they first entered upon the border lakes route to the West, through which the present international boundary winds its way.

From Grand Portage, which they reached in August 1731, having been joined at Michilimackinac by Father Mesaiger, La Vérendrye was himself ultimately to reach the distant Missouri, and his sons still more distant parts of its vast basin. But several years were to pass before these things were accomplished, and it is not the least remarkable feature of the group that the objectives of exploration should have been kept so long and so steadily before them. Indeed, long after they had lost favor at Versailles, and even at Quebec, the sons were yet to offer themselves for further exploration, in even the most humble capacity, still willing to complete the assignment that had been sought by their father.

La Vérendrye's bold plan of a chain of posts to Lake Winnipeg was soon to be realized. In the fall of 1731, La Jémeraye and one son built on Rainy Lake the first of these, Fort St. Pierre. La Vérendrye had remained at Kamanistikwia during that winter, but the following June he and his party proceeded to the new post and beyond, to Lake of the Woods, where he was present during the construction of the second of his new posts, Fort St. Charles. This fort was to become his new headquarters, taking the place of that at Kamanistikwia. Descriptions of both posts—dimensions, arrangement, and appearance—have been preserved, and the precise location of each is known.[21]

Again La Jémeraye was to act as his uncle's messenger to Quebec. In 1733 La Vérendrye sent him east to report in person on the western command. Accompanied by Mesaiger, and with the commandant's letters for the governor, La Jémeraye carried still another new map. From an extract of one of his letters, forwarded to France, we see that La Vérendrye still hoped that the expenses of exploration could be met from some source other than his own pocket.[22] But the minister sorely disappointed La Vérendrye, for his persistent suspicion is the most noteworthy feature of his attention in these matters.

We have information from documents carried to Quebec by La Jémeraye that La Vérendrye had been actively seeking further information on the western country. One of these documents, though a troublesome one historically, is of special importance. This is a "Map of a part of Lake Superior" (which actually shows a great deal more than the immediate region of that lake). Now in Paris, it may be the original carried down by La Jémeraye, forwarded there by Beauharnois with other papers.[23]

A note on his own tracing of this map by the archivist Margry—an expert witness—identifies a note on the original map as in the handwriting of Jacques N. Bellin—a second expert witness. This earlier note is of special interest since it reads "dressée par mr de la Jemeray" ("prepared by M. La Jémeraye"), and it preserves evidence of the increased knowledge of the West now in the hands of the explorers.

This new map makes it clear that La Vérendrye no longer believed, as he had in 1730, that the River of the West flowed out of Lake Winnipeg.[24] On this new map Lake Winnipeg is shown correctly as emptying into Hudson Bay. The River of the West, now a separate item, was to be reached overland from the Assiniboine River. Access to it is suggested by way of a *Chemin des guerriers* (Road of the warriors). Another legend preserves evidence of the inquiries that La Vérendrye had been conducting about the peoples living on the River of the West and provides one of their names, apparently for the first time: *Pais des Iskou à Chipouanes* (Country of the Iskou à Chipouanes). It is therefore certain that by 1733 the explorers had been told that the River of the West made a great bend near the villages of these people.

Beauharnois, having consulted with La Jémeraye and probably also with Mesaiger, and fully aware that exploration was now La Vérendrye's primary responsibility, planned the campaign for 1733–34 in "terms calculated to placate the Minister."[25] La Jémeraye was to start as soon as the ice melted for Lake of the Woods, where he might expect to arrive in August; in September he would set out once more, to winter 150 leagues farther on. The following spring, in 1736, he was to go to the country of the Ouachipouennes, otherwise called "The Sioux who go Underground."[26]

Beauharnois's letter contains further information on these new peoples, obtained from interviews with La Jémeraye. They lived on the River of the West some three hundred leagues from Lake of the Woods, according to Crees who had visited the region on war parties. The Crees stated that the Ouachipouennes had eight villages, with fields of Indian corn, melons, pumpkins, and beans; that they had horses and even cats; and that their dwellings were of wood and earth (*cabannes de bois et de terre*), built like those of the French. The Crees had of course seen the log buildings erected by La Vérendrye, adapted to materials at hand in the lake region, and the Cree comments on their similarity have some validity. That the new reports were more restrained than those first obtained may be inferred from the governor's remark that the new people were "of the same height as other Indians," and the observation that some of these people had light hair, some red, and some black is not too much to believe. That the Crees had heard an alien tongue in the West is witnessed by their statement that these people spoke a language that had some resemblance to French, but was quite unlike English. Such a statement was, of course, not so much factual as it was undoubtedly intended to interest the French.

Other Cree observations of these people record numerous cultural differences between themselves and these "Sioux who go Underground." The latter dressed in buffalo skins, used earthen pots, and had a few large axes, badly worn through use. The Crees said that these people never themselves made war on other tribes, but were always on their guard and defended themselves bravely when attacked. The Crees frankly admitted that they and the Assiniboins constantly made war on them and had even captured several of their children. Beauharnois wrote that Le Jémeraye had brought three of these children with him to Montreal. When these children saw cats and horses in Montreal, they said that they had animals of the same kind at home.

The Crees and the Assiniboins told La Jémeraye that they had made peace with the Ouachipounnes, and promised that they would guide him and La Vérendrye's son to their country, where they could obtain further information on how to reach the Western Sea, into which, it seemed, the great River of the West discharged. As a footnote to the information obtained, La Jémeraye said that he had spoken to about twenty Crees, individually in private and at different times, to see whether their accounts would agree, and that they had always told him the same thing. The only disagreement, he said, was with respect to certain animals the Indians had seen in their travels. The traders were obviously losing no opportunities to gather information that would be of help to them. If the court grew impatient, it was because it did not and could not appreciate the problems involved.

A number of documents dating after May 1733, in journal form, are available—doubtless based on actual field journals now lost. These documents, preserved in drafts forwarded to Paris, show that La Vérendrye continued to gather information on the West. In January 1734, he heard again of the new tribes living on the River of the West, from other native sources. This information, although obtained second-hand, was frequently corroborated by later personal observations by La Vérendrye and his successors. When, some five years later, he at last visited the upper Missouri River in person, he could not have been very surprised at what he saw there.

An important council was held with the Indians late in December 1733 at Fort St. Charles.[27] A number of Cree and Monsoni chiefs—members of tribes which La Vérendrye had previously interviewed—were at this council. Four Assiniboin chiefs were also in attendance. Because of their familiarity with the West, La Vérendrye found them to be good informants. Although he does not mention the fact, La Vérendrye must have been aware that the Assiniboins were especially well qualified sources, since they—like some of the people living along the Missouri River—spoke a Siouan language.

This council continued through the first few days of the new year, the commandant providing corn and fish for the all-important feast, remarking that "without the help of the pot you cannot have friendship." After the feast, and after having given gifts to the Indians, La Vérendrye began his inquiries once more.

The Assiniboins told him that as soon as spring came they would leave to visit the Achipoüanes to buy corn, as they had agreed to do. When in turn the Assiniboins were asked what they thought of the tribes along the River of the West, and whether they were Indians like themselves, the Assiniboins— like the Crees—replied that they took them for Frenchmen. Since the Assiniboins traded with the Mandans, they would scarcely have taken them for Frenchmen. The description that follows describes the Spanish settlements better than it does those of the Mandans. So, although La Vérendrye may have believed that he was obtaining a description of "civilized Indians," it seems more likely that he was obtaining a description of Spanish settlements in Texas or the Southwest. The Assiniboins would have known about the Spanish through their contacts with the Mandans.[28] These western peoples were, in fact, described as *Caserniers* ("Barrack-dwellers," or "Pueblos").

The Assiniboins said that the houses and forts of the westerners were much like those of the French, except that the roofs of their houses were flat and covered with earth and stone. Their forts were made of double rows of stakes *(leurs forts de pieux et bien doublés)*, and had two bastions, at opposite corners. The houses were large and had caches or storage pits *(des caves)* in which corn was kept in large baskets. The inhabitants, they asserted, never left the forts (that is, probably, to live elsewhere), and everyone, both men and women, worked in the fields, except for the chief.

These "barrack-dwellers" were tall, well proportioned, white, and walked with their toes "turned out." Their hair was sometimes light in color, chestnut or red, as well as black. The men had beards, which they cut or pulled out, though some allowed the beard to grow. These people were engaging and

affable with strangers who came to visit them, though they
remained on their guard. They did not visit neighboring tribes.
They were clothed in hides or in dressed skins that were
carefully worked and of different colors. They had a kind of
shirt *(Camisolle)* with breeches and leggings of the same
material, and their shoes seemed to be of one piece with the
leggings. Women dressed in long garments, a kind of tunic
reaching to the ankles, with a girdle having an apron, the entire
garment being of finely worked hide. They wore their hair in
tresses coiled on the head.

These people sowed quantities of corn, beans, peas, oats,
and other grains. These they traded with neighboring tribes
who visited their villages for the purpose. The women did not
work as hard as other Indian women, the Assiniboins thought,
but occupied themselves with domestic affairs and with keeping
things neat and clean. When work was pressing they helped in
the fields.

These westerners raised several different kinds of domestic
animals, such as horses and goats, and had domestic fowl,
including turkeys, hens, geese, ducks, and other varieties. Their
customary food was Indian corn, but they also ate a great deal
of the flesh of buffalo, moose, deer, and the like, which they
trapped in great pits covered with twigs and leaves. They
hunted on horseback, going out together to do so in groups.

La Vérendrye was told that the smallest forts of these
people were square and measured five or six arpents on a side—
approximately nine hundred or a thousand feet. They were
surrounded by a good ditch and had a stout gate *(porte doublé)*.
In the middle of each fort was a large space upon which all the
dwellings faced. All of the forts were on the banks of a stream,
and a subterranean passage led from the middle of this open
place to the edge of the water; thus the inhabitants could reach
the water and even embark without being seen. Their weapons,
both offensive and defensive, were bow and arrow, shield, axe,
and dart, the last of which was a kind of lance.

The house of the chief of each settlement, La Vérendrye
heard, was very large and higher than the rest, and occupied
the whole side opposite the gate. Within it, and at one end, were
the chief's quarters and those of his servants and slaves; the

central part was for public assemblies and the reception of strangers; the opposite end was assigned to his wives. This house had three principal entrances. Before the chief's dwelling was a pole with what he understood to be a weathervane *(giroüette)* on the top, while at the two ends of the house and raised above it were two buffalo skulls *(Têtes de boeüf)* with ornamental carvings, which La Vérendrye took to be the coats of arms of the tribe.

These westerners had but one great chief, he heard, under whom were a large number of separate forts, built on both banks of the great river. His informants knew of nine such forts, separated from each other by a league or less, but they had heard that there were a great many others, both upstream from and below that in which the principal chief lived. Each fort had its own chief, but all were subject to the first. When there was an alarm, the inhabitants could warn each other, from bank to bank, by means of a trumpet and in this way the entire nation could be put on the alert in a few hours, and they doubtless had other means of signaling.

The Assiniboins were particularly struck by the water-craft of these people, who had small boats made of hides. Rounded at the ends, they were propelled by one man using a double-bladed paddle or two small oars. Of the great river itself, they had seen that it was eighteen or twenty arpents wide, very deep, abounding in fish, and having a good current. They were not aware of any falls or rapids in its course. "It waters a vast mountainless country," La Vérendrye understood, "partly bare and in prairie, and partly in wood of a high growth, oak and other kinds of woods as in Canada."

Probably wondering how the Assiniboins could have learned so much of these westerners and of their country, La Vérendrye asked whether they understood the language. One Assiniboin told him that he had depended on an interpreter and had not stayed there long enough to remember any words of the language, but he insisted that they spoke and sang like the French.

La Vérendrye then asked about the tools these people used for cutting wood, and heard that they had no iron like that of the French. The Assiniboins were the only ones who traded with them—a few axes and knives, which they liked better than their own because they cut so much better, for corn. It was asserted that the axes which these people did have (and which they made themselves) were yellow and harder than copper. Their knives, made of the same material, were well made and fitted with deer antler handles. For kettles these strangers used pots of clay or earth *(pots de grais [glaise] ou de Terre)*, decorated on the outside and glazed on the inside.

Seeking still more information, La Vérendrye asked whether the westerners knew anything of the French. Some of the Assiniboins replied that they had been among them only four moons ago and had spoken to them about the French. This had pleased the westerners, and their great chief had asked the Assiniboins to tell the French chief that it would give them great pleasure to see the French and make friends with them. "If he comes himself, or if he sends one of his men," the chief was quoted as saying, "I beg him to let me know beforehand, in order that I may send to meet him as he deserves." Whether or not La Vérendrye was correctly apprised of the sentiments of the westerners, the western peoples had—if the account is to be believed—received notice of the impending arrival of the French.

It is not necessary to examine in detail the assertions of the Assiniboin informants at Fort St. Charles in 1734, for La Vérendrye did not repeat these observations in his own later documents after having visited the Mandans in their own villages, because he must have realized that the Assiniboins had been referring to the Spanish or he disregarded their statements as gross exaggerations.

Though he must have felt the urgency of making contacts with the new peoples along the Missouri River at the earliest opportunity, La Vérendrye announced, at the council of January 1734, that he would be unable to visit the Achipoüanes in less than a year's time. He had been away from home for more than three years, and most of his men were about to leave for Montreal for supplies. Although he had received supplies from home each fall, he was probably too poorly equipped at the time to make the push to the west at once.

The story of the La Vérendryes now takes a different turn, in part because of the tragic events that were now to befall. It is an often told story.[29] The ancient strife between the Sioux and other Indians of the region, especially the Crees and Monsonis in the border lakes region, was bound sooner or later to involve the French themselves. Distant native groups—defeated or exploited by those who were being supplied with white men's goods—could only regard the French as enemies, and would eventually find ways to break the encirclement by striking back at them.[30] The clash was inevitable, and La Vérendrye was to suffer directly and personally at the hands of the Sioux.

Late in the winter, La Vérendrye paid a visit to Fort St. Pierre to try to prevent the Monsonis from going to war against the Sioux. That spring, however, the Crees joined their relatives on the warpath and asked that his eldest son, Jean-Baptiste, go with them. At this time it is impossible to penetrate the motives of those concerned, but it is possible that Jean-Baptiste himself wished to go on such a foray. Consent was given by his father, probably reluctantly, but La Vérendrye offered as justification the fact that had he withheld his consent, the Indians would have taken the French for cowards. As Morton has shown, from the Fort Albany journal of the Hudson's Bay Company, it is likely that several French had been killed by the Sioux as early as 1734.[31] The commandant may have felt that the Sioux should now be chastened. If this was the case, however, the course proved disastrous. Quite aside from the loss of life that would ultimately result, explorations were further delayed and trade must have been severely curtailed. For Jean-Baptiste and Father Aulneau, as well as nineteen other Frenchmen, were later killed, probably by the Sioux—perhaps in partial retaliation for Jean-Baptiste's having accompanied the Crees and Monsonis against them in the spring of 1734.

Leaving his son Pierre in charge at Fort St. Charles, La Vérendrye left for Montreal on May 27, 1734. Meeting the Sieur Cartier, one of his merchant partners at Kamanistikwia, he sent him on to establish a post on the Red River. When he reached Michilimackinac he met La Jémeraye, returning from the East, and sent him on with orders to relieve Pierre at Fort

St. Charles, so that Pierre might help Jean-Baptiste build the new post on the Red River, to be called Fort Maurepas. This post—the first of two of the name—was a few miles south of the mouth of the Red River, probably on the small tributary called Nettley Creek.[32]

La Vérendrye probably returned to the settlements because of the expiration of his contract, as well as to refit. But for him the return, having gone no farther than Lake of the Woods, must have proven embarrassing to the governor, aware of the eagerness of the court for news of the River of the West and of the Western Sea. Beauharnois once more pleaded for royal assistance, but to no avail.[33] The River of the West was still unexplored, though more than three years had elapsed since the task had been assigned. It was in fact said that the officials in New France were not really looking for the Western Sea, but rather for "the sea of beaver."[34]

Beauharnois, in a much better position to understand the problems of the western command, did not fail La Vérendrye in his dispatches. "I venture to assure you," he wrote Maurepas, "that the zeal which he manifests for this enterprise cannot be suspected of any other motive than the well-being of the service and the colony, and that, up to the present, it has been a very costly thing for him."[35] Since the court, though finding fault with these efforts, had failed to suggest a practical means for explorations, the governor did as best he could to plan them himself. In order to free La Vérendrye from complete dependence on trade, he was now permitted to farm out his posts to various merchants for a three-year period. This was done in the expectation that the subletting would afford sufficient funds to carry on the search.[36] The new scheme further complicated La Vérendrye's tangled finances, but it provided that he himself should not have to do any trading, either directly or indirectly; thus, he would be able to pursue his goal of reaching the Sea of the West "with all possible diligence."

The governor's plans for the next campaign were also made plain to the ministry. La Vérendrye reported that he now had a post on Lake Winnipeg—assuming that his instructions were being carried out. This post, he thought, was only 150 leagues from the village peoples on the River of the West. He

was to depart in the spring of 1735 for his new post, Fort
Maurepas, and to arrange to go the following spring to visit
these westerners who, according to the Assiniboins, eagerly
awaited the opportunity to make an alliance with the French.
With him, La Vérendrye would take La Jémeraye and one of his
sons—probably Jean-Baptiste—who had an aptitude for Indian
languages. The son was to learn the language of the Ouat-
chipouennes, as the governor now spelled the troublesome
name. Acting as an interpreter, the son could obtain information needed to carry on the explorations. Still another
aide was to be added to La Vérendrye's staff at this time. His
youngest son, Louis-Joseph, now seventeen, who had so far
remained at home, was to be trained in mathematics and
drawing during the winter before the new departure so that he
would be prepared to make an accurate map of the country to
be explored.[37]

With the spring of 1735, the father was once more ready
to depart, and on June 6, together with his youngest son, he left
for the West. With him was yet another new participant, also
young and inexperienced in the problems now so familiar to the
commandant. This was Father Aulneau, whose brief career in
New France was to end in less than a year. Aulneau's letters to
his mother and to his fellow clerics afford a further record of
the Post of the North.[38]

As he was about to depart, Aulneau wrote that he was
being sent to carry the Gospel far into the unknown West,
among Indians "whom not one of us has yet set eyes upon." The
tribe, he wrote, had been given the name Ouant Chipouanes—
"those who dwell in holes"—and they had thus far remained
unknown to the rest of men.[39] In the best Jesuit tradition, he had
been instructed to have frequent conversations with these
people, by means of which he could learn their tongue and
thereby compile dictionaries of their languages. This he was
also to do for the Crees and Assiniboins, since so little was
known of them. But he was to remain only temporarily with
these two tribes: the Ouant Chipouanes, if reports were true,
lived in settled villages and there was consequently better
promise of doing good among them. Aulneau admitted that he
looked forward to his mission with "fear and trembling,"

especially since he would be alone among the tribe and far from spiritual assistance and support.[40]

It is clear from Aulneau's letters that the mission to the distant western tribe had been planned largely because of the settled habits of those people. The young priest had been well instructed in his duties and was in possession of what the order could learn of both the geography and the native tribes of the West. He had studied these matters carefully, and although he could not be certain, he concluded that the new people probably lived on the banks of the great Rio Colorado o del Norte, which his famous predecessor, Father Eusebio Kino, had shown on his map of California in 1705.[41]

Beauharnois had expected that La Vérendrye should go at least as far as Lake Winnipeg in 1735, and the following spring to the River of the West. But again, plans went awry. The commandant reached Fort St. Charles on September 6, 1735, and spent the winter there. The expected supplies, through the bad management of the guides, did not reach him that fall at all, and did not arrive in fact until the summer of 1736.[42] A fact La Vérendrye does not reveal, however, is that Fort Maurepas had not yet been built. In the fall of 1735 he sent Jean-Baptiste, and Pierre, with two men, from Fort St. Charles in that direction, probably to build the post that had been planned two years earlier. Whatever his reasons for not pushing on, La Vérendrye was still on Lake of the Woods at the beginning of the season of 1736, nor was he to see the distant West for more than two years.

Now he began to receive tragic news: on June 2, his two sons returned with word that La Jémeraye, his chief assistant for so long, was dead. He had died May 10 at the forks of the Roseau River—this is, probably, at the junction of the Roseau and the Red River. But the lonely death of his young assistant, of apparently natural causes, was but an omen of worse news to come. The supplies so badly needed had still not arrived from Montreal and, deciding not to wait for them, La Vérendrye sent Jean-Baptiste and a party to hasten them along. With them, returning to the settlements in the East, was Father Aulneau. Morton has said that Aulneau, in despair of succeeding with a mission to the nomads of the forest, had given up the task.[43] But his own letters show that his real objective had been the settled peoples of the great River of the West, and there is no hint of his having given up, or wishing to do so, in his letters.

While on their way from Fort St. Charles to Montreal, Jean-Baptiste, Father Aulneau, and their entire party—at least nineteen canoemen—were killed, perhaps by the Sioux, probably at a place long since known as Massacre Island, in what are now Canadian waters of the international boundary. Since none of the French party escaped to give a personal account, only the most lurid details of the massacre are known; even the details reconstructed in the months to follow are conflicting, down to the number of people killed. The details are, however, not really important here: the commandant and father sustained, as he said, "a blow from which he should never recover." Such a disaster "might well have stayed the steps of the most eager explorer," in the words of Morton, who suggests that the attack on the returning French party was nothing less than the answer of the Sioux to the arming of their enemies, the forest tribes, and to Jean-Baptiste's having taken up the warpath with them.[44]

Ironically enough, only a few days after this tragedy the long-awaited supplies reached Fort St. Charles with the arrival of a party under one of the merchant partners, the Sieur le Gras. For a time, all thought of the search for a Western Sea, and probably even of trade, must have been forgotten. Indeed, it was fall before La Vérendrye seems to have regained his composure. Not until September was he able to return to the matter of exploration, or even to send to the lonely island for the bodies of his son, the priest, and the men. When, however, this was accomplished, the remains were interred at the chapel at Fort St. Charles, where long afterward they were discovered and identified.[45]

Once more the sorely tried explorer took up his task. In September, he dispatched his son François, the Chevalier, with six men to Fort Maurepas at the request of the Crees and Assiniboins.[46] La Vérendrye had intended that his son go with Assiniboin guides to reconnoiter the country of the western villagers, and he provided the Chevalier, for the purpose, with a box of articles "such as might please these people," together

Fig. 2. La Vérendrye's 1737 manuscript map, based on Indian information. It was sent to Beauharnois before La Vérendrye had explored west of Lake of the Woods. (Courtesy of the Newberry Library, Chicago.)

with clothing, tobacco, axes, necklaces (or wampum), and even a French flag. The son was told to try to keep the Indians at peace and, among other things, to invite the western peoples to Fort Maurepas to form an alliance. But the son was unable to complete the mission because of the lack of canoes. Further explanations of the failure of this attempt are lacking, but the turmoil of the summer had probably brought no little fear to the hearts of the French.

Meanwhile, La Vérendrye continued his inquiries about the western country and its people. Those whom he had previously known as the Ouachipoüanes (the Monsoni term for them) he now learned were also called the Kouathéattes by the Crees. La Vérendrye now speaks of them as a race of men white in color, and civilized *(policés)*; it is evident that he is receiving dubious information on them.

Again the explorer asked his informants to prepare a map of the western country, and they did so. This map he forwarded to his superior. "You will see," he wrote Beauharnois, "that I have not forgotten the mines, nor whatever could aid in my explorations—tribes, rivers, mountains, etc." The map also has been preserved; its title reads "A map containing the new discoveries in the west of New France, seas, rivers, lakes, and nations inhabiting it in the year 1737" ("Carte contenant Les nouvelles découvertes de l'ouest En Canada, Mers, Rivières, Lacs, et Nations qui y habittent en L'année 1737").[47] Little attention is paid to scale, proportion, or orientation on this map, and it is obviously from native sources. When it was prepared, La Vérendrye had not gone beyond Lake of the Woods (fig. 2).

La Vérendrye was now conscious that the great river of the Ouachipouanes—or of the Kouathéattes—did not, as he had thought, flow to the west. Rather, it flowed to the south and finally discharged, apparently, into the Pacific Ocean. We may believe that Father Aulneau had discussed this matter with him, for La Vérendrye says that he was told there were white men, towns, forts, and cannon on this river, and prayers were said there by "black robes" (Jesuits) who lived in the country. His remarks suggest that he and the priest had been poring over Kino's map of the Southwest and the lower Colorado River. When he saw that the distance to the western people was no

more than some 150 leagues, La Vérendrye at last decided to
make the journey himself, believing that he would be able to
attain his objective by spring. But for one reason or another he
was unable to depart at once. He says that his men were afraid
to accompany him, an assertion that is easily believed after the
events earlier at Massacre Island.

On the new map he sent down to Quebec with his
memoir, La Vérendrye called the governor's attention to a
"height of land" indicated as a "mountain chain" running from
a point north of Lake Superior toward the unexplored new
region. Also worthy of note was a certain Rivière Blanche
(White River)—probably the Saskatchewan—which took its
rise in these highlands.

Beyond this height of land, the Crees said, they had
traveled as much as five days down the stream they called the
River of the West. They had been surprised to find there a
region having a quite different climate, and with different fruits
and trees, with which they were not acquainted. Once again,
some of their statements belong in the realm of folklore, but
some of them seem credible. For example, some of the nomadic
folk they mentioned were wanderers like the Assiniboins and
were known as the Pikaraminioüach. The name of this group
has proven to be indecipherable to students, but the description
of their customs leaves no doubt of the authenticity of the Cree
account, which relates to one of the numerous nomadic groups
on the northern plains.

The Pikaraminioüaches were very numerous, lacked
firearms, but like the Crees, had axes, knives, and cloth, which
they obtained from the lower part of the great river, where
white men dwelt in walled towns and forts. The Crees thought
the distance from the height of land to the sea to be perhaps
three hundred leagues, but they claimed to know no more about
these new people than they could learn from slaves they had
captured beyond the height of land. Their description ends on
the genuine note that the nomads in question carried their tents
or dwellings with them as did the Assiniboins. It is possible that
the Pikaraminioüaches were the people designated on the
accompanying map as *Hiatchiritiny*. The latter word is said to
mean "strangers" or "slaves" in Cree. Since the term was

commonly applied by the Crees to the Blackfeet, the map of
1737 may record the first French contacts (through the Crees)
with that important plains tribe.[48]

La Vérendrye remained at Fort St. Charles throughout the
winter and early in 1737 proceeded, for the first time, to the
new Fort Maurepas on the Red River. Here, on March 5, he
held another council with the Assiniboins and Crees. The
Assinboins again offered to guide him to the River of the West,
which they visited each year, but La Vérendrye once more
declined their offer. He says that he gave the lateness of the
season as his reason for not making the trip—"so as not to let
them think Frenchmen were afraid"—but adds that he planned
to return to Fort St. Charles, which he did not mention at the
council.[49] His farming leases would expire in 1738, and that
was probably his chief reason for not pushing farther west that
year, despite the specific instructions of his superior to do so.
The events of 1736 had caused more than a temporary delay.

During the council La Vérendrye had asked the
Assiniboins where they planned to spend the summer, and was
told that after raiding the Sioux they would go again to visit the
Kouathéattes to trade for corn and beans, for which they would
exchange the axes, firesteels, and other iron tools that those
people lacked. Making the most of the opportunity of this
contact, La Vérendrye entrusted to the Assiniboins the presents
he had intended to give in person to the Kouathéattes. The
Assiniboins promised to convey the gifts to them, together with
a message in the name of the governor. This message was to the
effect that the French wished to establish friendly relations with
the Kouathéattes and to enter into direct trade with them. La
Vérendrye went on to invite them to come in the fall to the
junction of the Red and Assiniboine rivers, where he planned to
build a fort so as to be nearer them. He wished them to come
with horses, bringing with them corn, beans, and some of the
metal they used, "particularly that which is the color of the
sun," as well as some of the stones that shone in the dark *(lüisent
la nuit)*, and other curiosities of which he had been told.

La Vérendrye had laid his plans for trade well in advance;
though he himself was soon to return to Quebec, he was
planning for future campaigns. The fort he promised the

Assiniboins he would build at the junction of the Red and Assiniboine rivers was not, however, to be built until the following year: it would be known as Fort Rouge.

When La Vérendrye returned to Montreal and Quebec in the fall of 1738, he must have been more than a little embarrassed at having to report that he had not yet visited the River of the West, which had now been his goal for more than six years. It was quite true that he had taken several long steps in that direction—at a cost that he alone could realize—and had accomplished much of the groundwork. He could point to the opening of the region from Kamanistikwia to the Red River and the establishment of three important new posts in that direction. No ministry could ever understand the effort necessary to accomplish these things. La Vérendrye may have felt that the task was too discouraging, too impossible to achieve, and he seems to have wanted to abandon it. In writing directly to Maurepas, he reported that he had for a time abandoned the explorations and asked to be given command of a company of troops at home.[50]

But Beauharnois had not thought of any such change; with unfailing constancy he supported La Vérendrye, sending to court, as before, the supporting evidence of his officer's papers and his new map. That Beauharnois, at least, had no notion of abandoning the search in the West is clear from his remarks that La Vérendrye had promised him that on his return to the West, in 1738, he would somehow get to the country of the Ouachipouanes, or Kouathéattes, and that a report would be in Beauharnois's hands no later than September 1739. Sympathetic though he was, the governor nevertheless reported that he had warned La Vérendrye "if he did not keep his word to me, I would call him back."[51]

The persistent minimizing of the accomplishments of the western command by the colonial ministry must have been extremely galling to governor and commandant alike. Failing to take due account of the character of the Indians, of the distances involved in the explorations, and of the sheer physical endurance and effort required—to say nothing of the unreasonable requirement that the explorer accomplish the king's pleasure at his own risk and expense—La Vérendrye's contemporaries, except for a few of his superiors at Quebec, seem to have ignored the quite remarkable achievements of his seven years in the West. History sheds a somewhat different light on the matter: the stage had been set for truly distant journeys. For the first time, groups of white men were to visit the drainage of the upper Missouri River, hitherto unexplored from that or any other quarter. The departure of La Vérendrye and his inexperienced group from Kamanistikwia in 1731 toward the border lakes country had been a first step toward this distant goal. Now a tired and wiser group took a strange new trail in the autumn of 1738, for the first time in their experience traveling overland on foot rather than in their trusted canoes.

3
Explorations of 1738–39 to the Missouri River: The La Vérendrye "Journal"

IN 1738, La Vérendrye at last set out for the country of the Ouachipouanes. The best account of this year-long venture— one of his own—is translated in this chapter. The manuscript is preserved in the Public Archives of Canada, to which it appears to have come from private sources, apparently from one Judge Badgley, who may have had the original through family descent. The text is not duplicated in official or private archives in France or elsewhere, although it must at one time have been copied for officialdom at Paris.

This translation is an abridgment, but it contains in full all of those parts bearing directly on the explorations southwest from Fort La Reine. For reference, page numbers (in brackets) are supplied for the unpaged original. The part of the account given here covers pages [4] to [20] of the twenty-two pages of the original; other parts are summarized in brackets.

This version has been prepared from the original manuscript and from photostats of the original. Three previous translations have been carefully studied.[1] The text is rendered literally, with a conscious effort to avoid interpolating ideas not clearly borne out by the text. The almost unbroken original narrative is divided into paragraphs, as has been done by two of the three previous translators.

Journal, in letter form, from July 20, 1738, the date of my departure from Michilimackinac, to May 1739; sent to M. the Marquis de Beauharnois, Commander of the Military Order of St. Louis, Governor and Lieutenant General of the whole of New France, lands and country of Louisiana, by his most humble servant La Vérendrye, lieutenant of a company of the detachment of marine in Canada, commissioned by his orders for the discovery of the sea of the west.

[1–3. With a party of twenty-two men in six canoes, La Vérendrye arrived from Michilimackinac at the *pais plats* (the Flat Country, a district near Kamanistikwia), on August 1, 1738. Here a brief council was held with the Indians, most of whom had gone to war with the Sioux. Kamanistikwia was reached on August 5, and here the governor's orders for this post and for Fort St. Pierre were left for Charles Nolan, the Sieur de la Marque, a trade associate who was expected shortly. The party left for Rainy Lake on the sixth. On August 22, they met a small band of Monsonis near the "little straits" of the lake and had a brief council with them. Fort St. Charles was reached on the thirty-first, and here, on September 3, another council was held with the Indians.]

[4] Having my youngest son received as commandant in my absence, and publishing an order to that effect, I departed on my journey, taking with me my other two sons. I delayed leaving until September 11 [1738], awaiting La Marque, of the trading company. I had earlier promised him that I would not hurry, thus giving him an opportunity to overtake me, and La Marque had promised, at Michilimackinac, to make all possible speed in order to accompany me in the fall in the proposed discovery of the Mantannes. These people have heretofore been called Ouachipouanne by the Monsonis, and Couatchouatte by the Crees; Mantannes is the proper name of the nation.

Since La Marque had not yet arrived by the tenth of the month, and everything being in good order at the fort as well as for my departure, I left the next day, still hoping that La Marque would overtake me in time to make the journey with me. Arriving at Fort Maurepas on the twenty-second, I held an inspection of arms, published your orders concerning the post, giving [a copy of them to] M. de Louvière, clerk for the trading company, and chose five men to go with me. As had been agreed, I left nine other men with de Louvière.

Reaching the forks of the Assiniboine River on the twenty-fourth, I found ten Cree families *(cabannes)* with two war chiefs, who were awaiting me with a large quantity of meat, having been notified of my coming. They begged me to remain with them for a while, to afford them the pleasure of seeing me and feasting us, and to this I consented, glad of an opportunity to talk to them.

[The council dealt with the attempt to prevent the Indians from trading with the English, with the feuds between the Crees and the Sioux, and with the death of Jean-Baptiste de La Vérendrye.]

A chief then asked where I planned to go. He said that the Assiniboine River was very low and that we would be running the risk of rendering our canoes quite useless. Furthermore, we would be among people who did not know how to take beaver, and clothed themselves only in buffalo hides *(peaux de beuf)*, which were not in demand, [5]—a people lacking good sense, who had never seen Frenchmen and would be unable to understand us.

I replied that during the fall I wished to visit the nation of white men of whom so much had been heard, and that I would ascend the river as far as I could go, in hopes of accomplishing the journey ordered by you. I stated that I wished to increase the number of your children, and to teach the Assiniboins how to hunt,—to teach them some sense;—another year I would go in some other direction.

The chief replied: "You are very likely, my father, to return with empty canoes. It is true that there are many Assiniboins, but they understand nothing of hunting beaver; I hope that you can teach them some sense."

[Encouraging the Crees to hunt diligently, to bring meat to the French post, and to keep their promises not to trade with the English, La Vérendrye again set out on September 26.]

I found the river very low, no rain having fallen during the summer. Its course is from the west, very winding and very broad, and having a swift current with many shallows; it is bordered with good timber along its banks and with prairies as far as the eye can reach, where there are many buffalo and deer. I decided to proceed by land, following the prairies, with the men I did not need following in canoes, and found the prairie route to be shorter, since it cut across several bends in the stream and one was thus able to keep a straight course. There is game along the river in great abundance.

I had not marched very far before meeting a number of Assiniboins, who had been told that I was coming up their river and had come to meet me. Keeping on my way, however, I put off talking to them until I should come to their own country. The party thus kept increasing every day. For six days I marched on, making good use of the time.

On the evening of October 2, the Indians warned me that I could ascend no farther, the river being too shallow to proceed in canoes. I was told that I had now reached the most favorable point on the river, both because of the abundant timber here, and for access to all the peoples of the region, situated as it was on the portage leading to the Lake of the Prairies [Lake Manitoba]. Here was the trail used by the Assiniboins in going to the English.

"If you were here," they said, "you could stop everyone. You wish to go to the *Mantannes*; here is the beginning of the trail."

I deliberated over what we should do. We estimated that we were now about sixty leagues from the forks [the junction of the Red and Assiniboine rivers] by water, and about thirty-five or forty by land, following the prairies. Everyone agreed that we could go no farther, and that to do so would be running the risk of rendering the canoes useless upon returning, and in a place lacking materials for refitting. Here there was neither pitch nor roots for that purpose. It would be better to remain here, where there was plenty of material for building. Here was the trail that led to the English, and here there was reason to expect many Indians, certainly all those who did not go to Fort Maurepas.

[6] I decided on the morning of the third to choose a suitable place at which to build a fort [Fort La Reine], and had it begun at once. I still hoped that La Marque would join me; if I were to go higher up the river La Marque would not be able to

find me. While the building was being pushed, I held a council with the Assiniboins. Assembling them all near my tent, I made them a present, on your behalf, of powder, ball, tobacco, axes, knives, chisels, and awls—all highly prized by them since they lack all such things. I was received with great ceremony and much weeping—evidence of their pleasure. In return for their trouble, I received them into the number of your children, following this with full instructions concerning your orders, repeated several times a day so that they would fully comprehend. This appeared to give them great satisfaction, and they thanked me heartily, promising to do wonders.

I ordered that the Assiniboins of the Red River also be notified that there were Frenchmen among them, who would not abandon them as long as they behaved sensibly; they should recognize your kindness to them in sending what they needed from such a great distance. Their kinsman, an old man I had brought with me, could tell them what had happened day by day. This man, on his part, spared no pains to inform them, and to demonstrate to them what it meant to have dealings with the French. The council was concluded with great weeping and hearty thanks from the Indians.

Several days later I secured a guide, whom, with others, I paid to accompany me on my journey and to carry my baggage. On the evening of the ninth, La Marque arrived with his brother, the Sieur Nolan, and eight men in two canoes. This pleased me very much, and I expressed my gratitude to La Marque for the trouble he had taken in bringing up reinforcements. I inquired of La Marque whether he had left a sufficient number of men at Fort St. Charles on Lake of the Woods, and how many he had left at Fort Maurepas. La Marque replied that he had left eight men at the first place with two traders, and had brought all his goods in his canoes, not with the expectation of being able to fill them all, since he was unable to bring any great quantity of goods, but because he had promised to join me and did not wish to break his word. He said that I would need men for the journey, and that he had brought them without loss to himself, since he would have no need of them during the winter.

I thanked him, observing that if he made no profit from

the journey, at least he and his men would be spared the expense
of the trip until their return. La Marque said that he wished to
share the expense, but I replied that this could not be. It was
sufficient that he should furnish men and himself go on the trip
without being at any expense; I had already provided for this.
At his request, I gave him a place in the fort on which to build a
house large enough to lodge all [7] his men upon returning from
our trip.

On the fifteenth, the fort and the houses having been
finished, I began making preparations for my departure. La
Marque informed me that he had brought de Louvière to the
forks, with two canoes, in order to build a fort [Fort Rouge], to
serve the peoples of the Red River. I approved of this, provided
that the Indians were notified.

On the sixteenth I had the long roll sounded for inspection
of everyone and selected those I would need for my expedition.
Following an inspection of arms, I caused your orders concerning the post to be read, and then detached twenty men—ten
of La Marque's and ten of mine—whom I ordered to be ready to
leave on the eighteenth. To each of them I issued a pound of
powder and twenty ball, with shoes *(souliers)*, an ax, and a
kettle for his use on the journey. To each man, both French and
Indian, I also gave a four-pound bag of powder, sixty ball, two
fathoms of tobacco, and various small goods such as awls, gun
flints, gun screws, and firesteels—more for their own needs than
anything else. In a leather bag were placed the goods I wished
to use as presents, and this bag our guide's wife carried for me.
Everything I needed for my own use was carried by my servant
and slave.

When this distribution was completed, I had Sanschagrin,
a man of good judgment, wise and prudent, who served as
sergeant under me, received as commandant in my absence,
taking my two sons with me. Leaving with Sanschagrin two
soldiers and ten *engagés* to guard the fort, I then gave him
orders and written instructions about everything he would have
to do during my absence.

On the eighteenth, everything being in good order at the
fort, I had all our party set out, ordering them to make camp
nearby. I and La Marque left about noon. Since the beaver were

not in season, I encouraged the Indians left at the fort to hunt buffalo in order to supply meat for the men I had left. Our small party consisted of fifty-two persons—twenty *engagés*, all good men, La Marque, his brother, my two sons, a servant and a slave; the rest were Indians.

The third day after our departure, a village of forty Assiniboin families overtook us with the intention of holding a council. The chief begged that I remain for a day to afford the Assiniboins the pleasure of seeing and feasting us. On the urging of the guide, I consented. Giving the chief a small present of powder, I repeated the statements I had made to all the rest. The chief was very grateful and made all sorts of promises; the Indians would take meat to the French [at the fort] and would hunt to the best of their ability in order that they [the French] might have what they needed.

On the twenty-first, we proceeded on our way, as far as the first mountain *(la première montagne)*, twenty-six leagues distant from our fort, going south by west *(sud quard [quart] de sudoüest)*; from the first mountain to the second *(la seconde)* going west by north *(oüest quard noroüest)*, twenty-four leagues. To go directly from the top *(pointe)* of the second mountain to the Mantannes we should have gone southwest by west *(sudoüest quard oüest)*. But we were unable to [8] follow a straight course; to make two or three leagues in a straight line we had to go three or four. From the fort the distance is probably 120 leagues west southwest *(oüest sudoüest)*, but our guide lengthened this by some 50 or 60 leagues and a number of stops, to which we were obliged to consent in spite of ourselves, letting the finest fall weather slip by encamped. Thus we spent forty-six days in accomplishing what we should have been able to do in sixteen or twenty days at most.

Of necessity we had to be patient. Nothing that I could say to the guide to make him hasten was of the slightest use. To crown our misfortunes, he took us twenty-two leagues off our route in order to reach a village of 102 families that he had gone to find. He brought back eight men, sent by the chiefs of the village to invite me to join them. They all wished to accompany me to the Mantannes and told me that the Sioux often visited the region and that I would need an escort. We had to resign ourselves to going there.

We arrived at this place on the afternoon of November 18. A number of scouts came out to meet us, and we were received with great joy. They led us—La Marque, his brother, and my sons—to the dwelling *(cabanne)* of one of the chiefs, where all was ready to receive us. A great feast was made for us and all the men, who did not lack a good appetite.

On the nineteenth I assembled the chiefs and head men of the village in the dwelling I occupied. On your behalf I made them a present of powder, ball, knives, and tobacco, telling them that I was receiving them into the number of your children, that if they behaved sensibly you promised not to abandon them, and that this day the French were established in their country and would provide them with all necessities. They, on their part, must hunt beaver and take good care of their own lands. At present you do not wish for war, but wish to pacify all the country, in order that your children may live in peace. To their number I was adding each day.

I made the same recital to them that I had made to all the others. There was a great display of gratitude, with profuse tears and the ceremony of placing their hands on my head, taking me in your place as their father and our Frenchmen as brothers, placing their hands on their heads likewise and weeping.

This ceremony ended, the village crier addressed me: "We thank you, my father, for having been willing to trouble to come to us. We shall accompany you to the Mantannes and will bring you back to your fort. We have already sent four men to notify the Mantannes. They have just returned, reporting that the Mantannes are very happy at the prospect of your going to them and will come to meet you. We have sent [9] four other young men to conduct them to a place we have selected. We will go slowly, hunting along the way in order to have fat on arriving, to eat with the Mantannes' corn. This they eat cooked with water, since most of the time they have neither meat nor fat."

I thanked them for their good-will and urged them to take

us there as soon as possible; they could see as well as I that the season was well advanced. Knowing that the Mantannes were not supplied with fat, I bought some in the village, giving all our party as much of it as they were willing to carry and having some carried for us by the Indians, who were paid for this. I informed our Frenchmen that I had in mind spending a part of the winter among the Mantannes and that they would need to be well loaded with fat; if they were not they would have to eat their corn and beans with water.

On the twentieth, the whole Assiniboin village set out on the march, to go seventeen leagues to the place of rendezvous with the Mantannes. Every day the Indians talked to us about the white men we were about to see—French like ourselves—who said they were descended from us. Everything we had heard gave hope of making a notable discovery. Along the way La Marque and I planned what we should do, especially what we should be ready to say, thinking the accounts true, though later we had to discount them greatly. I called La Marque's attention to the excellent order in which the Assiniboins marched to avoid being taken by surprise, going steadily over the prairies, hills, and valleys from the first mountain. The march never ceased to be fatiguing, ascending and descending many times a day. There were magnificent plains, three or four leagues in extent.

The marching order of the Assiniboins, especially when they are numerous, is in three columns, with some scouts ahead and on the flanks and with a good rear guard; the old and lame marched in the middle, forming a central column. I kept all the French together as well as I could. When, as often happens, the scouts catch sight of a herd of buffalo along the way, they raise a cry, which is at once carried to the rear guard. Then all the most active men of the columns join the vanguard to surround the animals. Having killed a number of them, each takes as much of the meat as he wishes. This is done without stopping the march. The vanguard choose the campsites, beyond which no one goes. They even make the dogs carry wood for fires, frequently being obliged to camp in open prairie, where the islands of timber are distant from each other.

On the morning of the twenty-eighth we reached the place chosen for meeting the Mantannes, who arrived toward evening, a chief with thirty men and the four Assiniboins. After the chief, from an elevation, had for some time examined the extent of the camp, which indeed made a fine appearance, I had him brought to my dwelling, at one side of which a place had been prepared to receive him. He came and seated himself near me. One [10] of his people who came in with him presented me with Indian corn in the ear and a roll of their tobacco, which is not very good because they are not familiar with preparing it as we do. It is very much like ours except that it is not planted [by hand] and is cut green, everything being used, blossoms and leaves together. I gave the chief some of mine, which he found to be very good.

I admit that I was surprised, having expected to see a people different from other Indians, especially in view of the account we had been given. They [the Mantannes] are not at all different from the Assiniboins; they go naked, covered only with a buffalo robe carelessly worn without a breechcloth. I knew by this time that we would have to discount everything we had been told about them.

The chief spoke to me in Assiniboin, expressing to me the pleasure my arrival among them would afford all their people. He begged me to admit them to the number of your children, and desired hereafter to be united with us; he said that I might dispose of all that he had. The chief begged me to stay at his fort, which was the nearest, smaller than any of the rest but well supplied with food. He said that there were six forts belonging to this nation; his was the only one somewhat removed from the river. The chief had received two necklaces *(colliers)* from me, which would be shown me on arriving at the fort. These people had always hoped to see me, said he.

I thanked him for all his attention and offers, saying that I had come a long way in order to establish friendly relations with them and that I would address them as soon as I arrived at their fort.

The chief at once played a trick on us. Having examined our camp on his arrival, as I have said, he foresaw that there would be a great company if everyone went to the fort. This would entail a great consumption of corn, their custom being to provide food freely for all who visited them, selling only the corn taken away. The chief gave the Assiniboins profuse thanks for having brought the French to them, saying that they could not have come at a better time, for he had been warned that the Sioux were about to arrive. He begged us, as he did the Assiniboins, to be good enough to give help, greatly relying on our valor and courage.

Like the Assiniboins, I fell into the trap—with this difference, that the Assiniboins were left dumfounded, whereas I was much pleased, thinking I had found an opportunity to avenge myself on the accursed Sioux. I promised him every assistance if the Sioux came while we were with them, both for myself and for all our Frenchmen, and for this the chief thanked me. He was then invited to a feast and questioned by the Assiniboins about the Sioux. The Assiniboins, though numerous and strong and hardy men, are not brave; they greatly fear the Sioux, whom they consider brave. The Mantannes know their weakness and profit by it on occasion.

A council was held to decide what should be done. The majority vote was that they should go no farther, and that I should be warned the risk I would run if I still wished [11] to continue.

An old man rose and spoke vigorously. "Do not think our father a coward," he said, "I know him better than you do. I have been with him since he left his fort. Don't imagine that the Sioux can frighten him or any of his men. What will he think of us? He has gone out of his way to reach us, assenting to our demand to accompany him to the Mantannes and to guide him again to his fort. He would have reached there today if he had not listened to us, and now you are thinking of abandoning him and letting him go on alone. This shan't happen! If you fear the Sioux, let us leave our village here until our return, and let all the men able to march follow our father."

Everyone agreed with the old man's opinion. It was decided that only a few men should remain, to protect the women; all the rest would accompany me. I was told of the result of the council. Word was sent throughout the village to warn everyone to be ready to march the day following, the thirtieth of the month. This afforded the Mantannes an opportunity for profit, by trading their corn, tobacco, buffalo hair *(poilles)*, and dyed feathers, which they knew the Assiniboins value highly. The latter had brought muskets, axes, kettle, powder, ball, knives, and awls to trade. The Mantannes are much craftier in trade, as in everything else, than the Assiniboins, who are always being cheated by them.

We left on the morning of the thirtieth, about six hundred men and several women without children, the best walkers. On the evening of the third day of our march, when about seven leagues from the first fort of the Mantannes, I was told that an Assiniboin had taken the bag from my slave along the way, under pretext of relieving him, and had returned to the village. My box, containing my papers and many other things needed, was in this bag. I immediately hired two young men to run after it and paid them, making them promise to bring the bag to me at the Mantannes, where I would wait for them. They set out during the night and overtook the rascal, who had already fled from the village. They made him return everything, but then returned to the village, keeping the property and expecting to restore it to me on my return, but not daring to come to find me for fear of the Sioux. Thus I found myself deprived of things very much needed.

The crier announced that we must leave before four o'clock in the morning in order to arrive in good time at the fort. About noon, a league and a half from that place on a small river, I found a large number of people who had come to meet us and had lighted fires while awaiting us. They had brought boiled corn and meal cooked with pumpkin, enough food for all of us. Two chiefs had made a place for me near a fire and gave me something to eat and something to smoke. La Marque arrived soon after me, [12] and I invited him to sit nearby and eat while he rested.

We remained there resting fully two hours. Then I was informed that it was time to go. I had one of my sons carry the flag, painted with the arms of France, and march at the front, and ordered the French to follow in marching order. Nolan relieved my son in carrying the flag, each in turn. The Mantannes would not allow me to walk, but insisted on carrying me. I had to consent, being urged by the Assiniboins, who said that it would cause much dissatisfaction if I refused.

At four arpents [about 50 rods or 275 yards] from the fort, on a small hill, a party of old men of the fort, accompanied by a great number of young men, were awaiting me, to present the calumet and to show me the two necklaces I had sent them four or five years previously. I and La Marque were given a seat. I received their compliments, the substance of which was the pleasure they felt at our arrival. I ordered my son, the Chevalier, to have all our Frenchmen draw up in line, the flag four paces distant in front; all the Assiniboins who had muskets placed themselves in line like the French. After returning their compliments, I caused three volleys to be fired in salute to the fort. A great number of Indians had come to meet us, but it was nothing compared to the number who appeared on the ramparts and along the ditches.

We marched in regular order to the fort, which I entered December 3 at four o'clock in the afternoon, escorted by all the French and Assiniboins. We were led to the dwelling of the head chief, which though large was not large enough to hold all who wished to enter. The crowd was so great that the Assiniboins and Mantannes trod on each others' heels. There was room only where we were—La Marque, his brother, and my sons. I asked that the crowd be made to leave, to make room for the Frenchmen, and that they put the baggage in a safe place, telling them that there would be plenty of time to see us. Everyone was cleared out, but not soon enough, for the bag of goods containing all my presents was stolen, through the great neglect of one of our *engagés*, in whose care it had been placed before reaching the fort. On entering the dwelling he had put down his load without paying much attention to the bag, which he had put beside him in the dense crowd. I found myself considerably inconvenienced—my box lost and my bag of presents, very much needed here and worth [13] more than three hundred livres.

The Assiniboins seemed very much distressed and made a great search at once, but to no avail. The fort is full of caches *(caves)* in which it is easy to hide anything. The chief of the

Mantannes appeared to be greatly troubled at my loss and to console me told me that there were a great many rascals among them, but that he would do all he could to find out something. Had I wished to avail myself of the offer of the Assiniboins to use force, I might have found something, but I preferred to suffer loss and keep everything quiet, since I wanted to spend a part of the winter among them in order to learn more of the country beyond.

On the fourth, I had the Mantannes and Assiniboin chiefs assemble in the dwelling where I was staying. I made them my present of powder and ball, telling them that I was unable to give them anything else. They knew that everything I had brought to give them had been taken from me. I declared that I intended to remain for a while to learn more of the region, in accord with your orders, and this could not be done in a day. The Mantannes expressed satisfaction at this, assuring me that I need not fear running short of food. They had food in reserve, more than I would need. Their forts were all well provisioned, and I might dispose of this food since I was master there.

One of the older Assiniboins, the village crier, said to me "My father, we have brought you here, and I do not doubt that here you will be well cared for. We had hoped to take you back to your fort, but you are master and may do what you think best. We shall come again to get you whenever you wish." Then, addressing the Mantannes, he said: "We are leaving our father with you; take good care of him and of all the French. Learn what he can teach. He is a spirit; he knows how to do everything. We love and fear him; do you as we do. We are leaving, much grieved at the theft committed against our father on coming among you. What must he think of you? You cannot deny that it is a shameful thing—the Frenchman comes to see you and you rob him. You do not understand who it is you are speaking to. It is very fortunate for you that our father is good-natured, or things would not have turned out as they did. I am not afraid to tell you that he could have made you find the bag had he wished—and there is still time to do so if he wishes."

Here I made him stop speaking, seeing that the old man was beginning to lose his temper.

One of the chiefs of the Mantannes replied: "Neither I nor

any of my people had any part in what you accuse us of; I do not speak for any of the rest. I am very sorry for what has happened. I have had my young men search everywhere and have nothing to reproach myself about. Who knows if it wasn't an Assiniboin? There were some of both tribes in the great crowd. You can't answer that. You needn't be concerned about our father or his party. He is master here as he would be at home, and we pray that he will number us among his children."

This I did at once by placing my hands on the head of each chief—the customary ceremony. They responded with great shouts of joy and thanks. I then said to the Assiniboins: "I am sending four Frenchmen to my fort to give news of me. I ask you to take them there as soon as you can. I left powder at the village and everything needed [14] to take them there." The council then ended with profuse thanks on all sides.

But the Assiniboins did not yet talk of leaving, though they had purchased all they could afford, such as the painted buffalo robes, hides of deer and antelope (chevreuille), well dressed and decorated with hair and feathers, dyed feathers, hair, garters, head bands, and belts. They [the Mantannes] dress hides better than any other people, and do work in hair and feathers very pleasingly; the Assiniboins are unable to do as well. They are sharp in trading, stripping the Assiniboins of all they possess, such as muskets, powder, ball, kettles, axes, knives, and awls.

Seeing the great consumption of food made each day by the Assiniboins, and fearing that they might stay a long time, the Mantannes started a rumor that the Sioux were near and that several of their hunters had seen them. The Assiniboins fell into the trap and quickly made up their minds to decamp, not wishing to have to fight. A Mantanne chief, by a sign, made me understand that the rumor about the Sioux was merely to make the Assiniboins leave. On the morning of the sixth they all departed in great haste, thinking that the Sioux were nearby and fearing lest they fall upon them along the way.

The chief with whom I had lived in the Assiniboin village brought five men to stay with me, saying: "My father, I am sorry to leave you. I still hope that you will join us in a little while, and I shall travel slowly. Here are five of my young men, whom I give to remain here with you. They will bring you along whenever you wish to leave."

I gave him a small present, by way of thanking him, saying that he would soon be aware that I was grateful and intended to reward him for his attentions. The chief then left, with great protestations of friendship.

Shortly afterward, I was notified that our interpreter, whom I had paid well to ensure keeping him, had run away despite all the offers my son the Chevalier had made to him, and was following an Assiniboin woman he had become enamored of but who would not consent to stay with him. He was a young man of the Cree nation who spoke good Assiniboin. There are several Mantannes also who speak this language very well. Thus I could easily make myself understood; my son spoke Cree and the Crees interpreted in Assiniboin.

But now, to crown our misfortune, we were reduced to making ourselves understood by means of signs and gestures. Had I distrusted the interpreter, who assured me daily that he would [15] always remain with me and never desert me, I should have profited by the time he was with me to ask the questions I wished to put to the Mantannes. But, flattering myself that I had a man on whom I could rely, I had put off doing so until after the departure of the Assiniboins.

I was much hampered all day. All I was able to find out I learned from the few questions I asked in the evening after almost everyone had withdrawn, such as whether there were many people along the river, descending, and what tribes, and whether they had any knowledge of more distant places. I was informed that there were five forts belonging to their nation *(nations)*, on the two sides of the river, much larger than that in which we then were. At a day's journey from the last of their forts are the Panaux, who have several forts; then come the Pananis. These two tribes hold a large region, but are at war with the Mantannes and have been for the last four years. Formerly these tribes were always closely united and in alliance with each other. They said that they would later tell me the causes that had set them at odds. The Panana [sic] and Pananis build their forts and dwellings as do the Mantannes and in summer have corn and tobacco.

The lower part of the river, I was told, is so wide that from one side one cannot see land on the other and the water is unfit to drink. All these regions are inhabited by white men like ourselves, who work iron. The word *iron* among all these tribes of this region means all kinds of metals, called iron. These white men travel only on horseback, both for hunting and for war. They cannot be killed with arrow or musket, because they are covered with iron, but by killing the horse one can catch the man easily, since he cannot run away. They have bucklers of iron, very light in color, and fight with lances and sabers, in the use of which they are very skillful. Women are never seen in the fields. Their forts and houses are of stone.

I inquired whether there were any forests and whether the prairies extended on all sides, in hills and valleys. The Indians replied that along the river were woods here and there, and also on the prairies, in clumps of timber. The farther one descended the river, the greater were the slopes, many of which were bare bluffs of fine stone, especially along the river.

I asked if it took very long to reach the white men, the horsemen, and was told that the Panana and Pananis had some horses like the whites. It would take the Mantannes a whole summer to make the journey, even if only the men made the trip. But because they are at war with the Panana they would not dare go very far, the trails being closed to them. They said that the buffalo were abundant on the prairies, far larger and fatter than most of those we had seen there, the hair being white or of several colors. They showed us some horns split in half that hold nearly three pints and are of a greenish color. There are some of these in all the dwellings and they serve as ladles— proof that the Indians have killed many at times when the trails were open. This was all I could learn, and that by chance, having depended on having my interpreter and on having ample time to inform myself fully, at leisure.

On the sixth, after the departure of the Assiniboins, I sent my son, the Chevalier, with Nolan, six Frenchmen, [16] and several Mantannes to the nearest fort, which was on the bank of the river. If they were well received they were to stay overnight, to inform themselves as best they could concerning the direction of the river on which this people lived and whether they had knowledge of the lower part in accord with what we had already been told. They were to learn all they could about it, as best they could by signs and gestures.

After their departure La Marque and I walked about to see the size of their [fort and] fortifications. I gave orders to have the dwellings counted, and it was found that there are probably as many as 130. All the streets, open places *(places)*, and dwellings are similar, and some of our Frenchmen often lost their way among them. The streets and open places are kept very clean, and the ramparts are smooth and broad. The palisade is braced with crosspieces mortised to the posts fifteen feet apart, with a lining *(quinze pieds à quinze points doublé)*. Green hides, fastened at the top, are hung for lining where needed, as in the bastions. There are four such bastions at each curtain, well-flanked. The fort is built on a height in open prairie, with a ditch more than fifteen feet deep and fifteen to eighteen feet wide. The fort can be entered only by means of steps *(des marches)* or timbers *(des piesses)*, which are removed when there is danger from the enemy. If all their forts are similar to this one, they may be called impregnable against Indians. Their fortification is not at all Indian-like.

This nation is of mixed blood, white and black. The women are fairly good-looking, especially the light-complexioned ones; many of them have blond or fair hair. They are a very industrious people, both men and women. Their dwellings are large and spacious, and are divided into apartments by broad planks. Nothing is left lying about, all their belongings being kept in large bags hung from the posts. Their beds are made like tombs, surrounded by hides. Everyone sleeps naked, both men and women. The men go completely naked all the time, except for a buffalo robe covering. A great part of the women go naked like the men, with the difference that they wear a small, loose loincloth, about a hand-breadth wide and a span long, sewed to a girdle in front. All the women have this kind of covering even when they wear a skirt, so that they are never embarrassed or keep their legs closed when they sit down, as all other Indian women do. Some of them wear a kind of shirt of antelope hide, well softened. There are many antelope here, a very small animal.

Their fort has a great number of caches, in which they keep everything they have, such as corn, meat, fat, dressed robes, and bearskins. They are well supplied with these things, the currency of the region. The more they have the richer they consider themselves. They are fond of tattooing, but never more than half the body is marked, for either men or women.

They make wickerwork very skillfully, both trays and baskets. They use earthen pots that they make, like many other nations, for cooking food. They are for the most part [17] great eaters, and are very fond of feasts. Every day they brought me more than twenty dishes—corn, beans, and pumpkins, all cooked. La Marque, who did not dislike feasts, attended them constantly, with my sons. Since I did not go to them, my share was sent to me.

The men are large and tall, very active, and the greater part fairly good-looking. They have fine features and are very affable. Most of the women do not have Indian features. The men play a kind of ball game *(joux de boule)* on the open spaces and ramparts.

Nolan and my son returned on the evening of the seventh, well pleased with their journey, having been well received and strongly urged to remain longer. They reported to me that the fort is on the bank of the river and once again as large as this one. The open places and streets are very fine and clean. The palisade and fortification there are in better condition, the whole built in the same style as that in which we were. From all they could learn, all the forts are alike—to see one is to see them all, except that some are much larger than others. The farthest is the largest of all and nearest to the Pananas. According to the compass, the river appears to run southwest by south *(sudoüest quard de sud)*; by signs they were made to understand that the lower part probably runs to the sea southwest by west *(sudoüest quard ouest)*. The Indians often interrupted the conversation; not being able to understand the questions asked, they answered about other things because they did not comprehend.

The waters of the river run very rapidly, and there are many shallows. The water is not good to drink, being somewhat brackish. Since leaving the last mountain, we have everywhere found almost all of the marshes and ponds brackish or sulfurous. All they could understand was that there are men like ourselves on the lower part of the river who make woolen stuffs and linen. They are very numerous and carry on wars with a great number of Indians.

"We saw that it was useless to attempt to question the Mantannes further, since they could not understand us," [the two reported]. "We did not stop going to the feasts all the while we remained at their fort but still could not attend all to which we were invited. We noticed that on the prairies there are several small forts containing forty or fifty dwellings, built like the larger forts. These are uninhabited at present, and we were given to understand that the Mantannes go there during the summer to work their fields, and that they have a great deal of corn in the caches, in reserve." This was all the information the two could give me from their visit.

On December 8, I had my son observe the elevation [of the sun] *(prendre hauteur)*, which he found to be forty-eight degrees and twelve minutes. I had consulted with La Marque the evening of the seventh about what we should do. He knew, as I did, that there were few things left for presents and that this made it impossible to continue any farther. The season was too unpleasant to undertake anything more. Above all, there was no interpreter, nor any hope [18] of obtaining one during the winter. We had good reason to fear that the trails would become impassable in the spring because of high water, according to report, and [that we] should be in danger of arriving after the departure of the canoes [eastward]. The powder I had left would probably not be sufficient to provide for all our needs during the course of the winter. Considering the few trade goods that remained, we might find ourselves much inconvenienced with so many men, since there was no longer anything to pay for guides. The Indian will give service only as long as he is paid, and in advance, and considers promises a subterfuge. On the other hand, we had reason to hesitate setting out on a march in the most inclement season of the year.

Taking everything into consideration, we decided that we must go, leaving behind only two men capable of learning the language of the Mantannes quickly. One was left in the fort where we were staying, and the other in the next nearest fort. Being alone, each would learn much more quickly and could later give us every kind of information. La Marque chose one of his *engagés*, a man of intelligence and one of his best men, who knew how to write. I gladly accepted him and gave him as assistant my own servant, although he was very useful to me and was very much attached to me personally. I preferred to deprive myself of his services, considering the help he would later be. I knew him to be a man of quick wit, good memory, having a great aptitude for language, and very wise and God-fearing. I gave these men full instructions on all they had to do, and La Marque, on his part, promised to send for them during the course of the coming summer.

Having thus arranged for the two men I was leaving behind, I notified our five Assiniboins, making them understand that I wished to leave shortly. This pleased them greatly. Not being able to make myself understood otherwise, I directed by signs that the following morning two of them leave with the two Frenchmen, and that everything should be made ready to go quickly to their village to warn the Indians there to expect us; I would leave four days after their departure, and was going to prepare for my journey. I then made known to the Mantannes my plan, which seemed to grieve them very much. Pointing out the two Frenchmen I was leaving in my place, I asked that they be well taken care of. The Indians thanked me heartily with great protestations of friendship and fidelity. I made them understand by this action that I would not abandon them. I asked the chief to provide cornmeal for our journey.

The news soon spread throughout the fort. On the morning of the eighth I had the two Frenchmen set out, guided by the two Assiniboins, as has been said, to go to the Assiniboin village to notify them of my own departure. Cornmeal was brought me during the day, much more than I needed. I thanked the Indians and gave them some [19] needles, which they value highly. They could have loaded a hundred men for me very quickly in the course of the day; everyone was eager to bring me what was needed. I had each of our men take as much of the corn as he would, and this was done in a very short while. Having provided everything that would be needed by all of our men, I had the chiefs and head men of the Mantannes assemble and gave them a present of powder, ball, and several small articles they valued highly because of their lack of them.

I gave the head chief a flag and a lead tablet, which I had decorated with ribbon at the four corners. This tablet was placed in a box, so that it might be kept forever, in memory of my having taken possession *(prise de possession que je fesois)* of their lands in the name of the king. It will be well guarded, from father to son—better than it would if I had buried it in the ground, where it might have been in danger of being stolen. I made them understand as best I could that I was leaving them this token in memory of the visit of the French to their country. I should greatly have liked to make myself clearly understood and to talk to them about things that would be of advantage to them and to us, but that was not possible, to my great regret and to theirs.

I had labored so diligently that by the evening of the eighth everything was ready for our departure, which I now found could be made sooner than I had previously planned. I fell sick, however, on the night of the eighth and ninth and soon was very sick. I did not know what to think of this. I kept to my bed for three days, and finding myself much better on the fourth, prepared to leave the next day. I gave the two men I was leaving enough to defray their expenses liberally, and even to pay for a guide if they should need one to bring them back to our fort. I also informed them once more of the reasons that obliged me to leave them there. As soon as they could make themselves understood, they were to overlook nothing to learn who this nation of white people were, what this iron was that they worked, whether to their knowledge there were any mines, what nations were above as one ascended the river, and if they knew of a height of land—in short, to overlook nothing in obtaining all possible information on the country.

On December 13, to the great regret of all the Mantannes, I set out, though ill, in the hope that my illness would not be serious and that in the [Assiniboin] village I would recover my box, in which I kept some medicines. A chief came to accompany us for a league and a half, from which point I sent him back. He made a great display of the regret he felt at my leaving, making a sign to ask me not to abandon him but to return, and that he would accompany us. I gave him a small amount of powder, once more asking that he take good care of the two Frenchmen I had left with them. The chief made a sign that he could take one of them into his own family, and I sent him off, having thanked him heartily.

That evening I noticed that there were only two Assiniboins with us. They explained to me that one of them had remained with our Frenchmen, not wanting to leave them, and that he would not return until summer, with them.

I reached the Assiniboin village on the twenty-fourth, still very sick. We had met with excessively cold weather, which caused us much delay. My box was restored to me, nothing in it having been touched. [20] The thief had been satisfied with the slave's bag, which was returned to me empty. When I had rested a little, I reproached the Assiniboins for having lied to me about the Mantannes; in all that they had told me I had found very little truth. They answered that they had not intended to refer to the Mantannes in saying that "they" were like us, but meant the people lower down the river, who worked iron.

An Assiniboin rose above the rest and said to me: "I am the only one here who can speak well about these things. You have not understood clearly what was said to you. I do not tell lies. Last summer I killed one of the people, who was covered with iron, as I have many times told before this. If I had not first killed the horse, I could not have got the man."

I asked him: "What booty of his have you brought back, to show us that you are telling the truth?"

To this he replied: "As I was about to cut off his head I saw some men on horseback who were blocking my retreat. I had a great deal of trouble to save myself, and could not keep anything to bring away. I threw away everything I had, even my robe, and ran away naked. What I am telling is true and I shall have it repeated to you next you shall see them. What I have just said I shall repeat to you. One cannot see the other side of this river. The water is salty. it is a country of mountains, with great valleys between them, of very find land. There are many buffalo, fat and large, white and of different colors. There are many deer and antelope. I have seen their corn fields; no women are to be seen in them. What I am telling you is without deceit; you will learn more about it in the future."

After three days' rest, I resumed my journey. I reached the first mountain on January 9 [1739], and here we camped for a long time. Seeing that I was still very sick, La Marque decided to go on ahead, with the purpose of sending me aid. He arrived [at Fort La Reine] on the first of February, I not until the tenth, greatly fatigued and very sick. At thirty-five leagues from the fort, I received the help he had sent, which I appreciated very much, being in great need of it. Never in my life have I endured so much misery, sickness, and fatigue as I did on this journey. After two weeks' rest I found myself somewhat recovered.

[La Marque went on to Fort Maurepas on March 16, leaving his brother and a large number of his men at Fort La Reine. Provisions were nearly gone, there being forty-two persons there, but the shortage was supplied by Indians who appeared there. La Marque wrote on April 16 that he had seen no Indians and was in despair.

[21. La Vérendrye sent the Chevalier on April 16 to explore the vicinity of Lake Winnipeg and the Saskatchewan, where he himself planned to go on the return of the convoy in the fall. The Chevalier was to obtain information about mines, make a circuit of the lake, and try to prevent the Indians from going to the English by making them hope for his father's early arrival there. A letter received from La Marque on April 23 said that no Indians had yet been seen, and that he had decided to go in search of them on the Winnipeg River. Learning that a great band of Assiniboins were camped on Lake Manitoba, making canoes for the English, La Vérendrye sent Sanschagrin with an *engagé* to bring them in. Five of the Assiniboins arrived on April 30 with news that many of the tribe were coming; only a few of them actually arrived, however, when they appeared on May 3. Nolan left on May 10, though La Vérendrye thought it unfortunate that he depart empty-handed. Other Assiniboins arrived on May 18 for brief trading, and others were expected shortly.]

I [have] discovered during this brief period a river that runs to the west. All the rivers and lakes of which I have any knowledge run toward Hudson Bay, the north sea, except this river of the Mantannes. I shall obtain complete information about this river this summer, either myself or through someone acting on my behalf.

[La Vérendrye delayed the eastbound canoes until May 28, waiting uselessly for the Indians, only a few of whom appeared. They had thought he would wait all summer for them, [22] but he assured them that as soon as his son and the two men he had left with the Mantannes returned, he would depart at once.]

4

An Interpretation of the
La Vérendrye "Journal"

THERE are many ambiguities in the account given in the last chapter, and it is our purpose in this chapter to offer an interpretation of the route traveled by the La Vérendrye party and specific comments on a variety of subjects mentioned in the account, to better understand La Vérendrye's activities on the occasion of this first visit to the Mandan villages along the Missouri River. The interpretation makes no pretense of being definitive, and continuing scholarship will bring many further refinements to the comments offered here.

The manuscript from which the previous chapter was translated is not of the primary character needed for historical certainty. It is, however, the only circumstantial account extant of La Vérendrye's activities during the years 1738 and 1739, when the upper Missouri River basin was first entered. Almost without exception, nevertheless, the document has been inaccurately referred to as *the* "journal" of the period. Although the account relates events and activities in chronological order, the manuscript is not in fact a field record—that is, with entries made from day to day at various places on the trip. Rather, it is a letter in journal form; not an actual letter sent, but a draft of such a letter. Nor does it appear to be an official draft, for it is neither in La Vérendrye's handwriting nor signed or endorsed by him.

A comparison of the manuscript with known examples of his handwriting clearly demonstrates that the writing is that of another person, perhaps a professional clerk. The narrative is smooth and flowing, as though the writer were copying from another document, and is relatively free from errors and corrections such as might have been made by a copyist. Parkman referred to the account as "ill-written and sometimes obscure," but his statement can only have been made from a study of the first printed text, that of Douglas Brymner, which was unskillfully edited and badly translated.[1] Inasmuch as the manuscript is not signed, bears no corrections in his hand, and does not even carry La Vérendrye's name at its end, it is possible that he never even saw the draft. Had he reviewed the manuscript, we could expect corrections from him and that he would have signed his name to it.

It would be important to know whether the original letter, the draft of which has been preserved, was actually sent to and received by the governor. This information would materially assist in establishing the authenticity of the document. Unfortunately, no such letter is known, either in archives in Paris or in Canada. Had the original been forwarded to Paris by the governor, it might be among the voluminous papers of the period extant there. If the original remained among personal or official papers of the governor in New France (or in France itself, to which Beauharnois retired), the original is not now known. The destruction of the archives at Quebec by various fires in the eighteenth century may well explain the lack of the original letter in Canada.

Can anything be learned of such a letter from those documents that do survive? From evidence in the draft itself, it would appear that the original was composed (or completed) about May 28, 1739, since the last event mentioned is the departure eastward of the canoes on that date. Precisely when this party reached Montreal and Quebec is not known, but the letter, if sent, would doubtless have been transmitted by this means.

On August 14, 1739, Beauharnois, writing to Paris, said that he had received no recent news concerning La Vérendrye.[2] The governor nevertheless says he "has been assured" that La Vérendrye had reached the Indians called the Blancs Barbus (Bearded White People), hitherto unvisited. It is curious that Beauharnois, in writing Maurepas, should confuse Indians with whites; La Vérendrye would not now have perpetuated this misunderstanding, nor would he have claimed to have reached any whites.

Sometime after August 14, however, Beauharnois did receive news of La Vérendrye's recent activities. He included this information in a dispatch dated October 6, 1739, which refers to a letter he had received from La Vérendrye dated May 28.[3] But the governor did not quote from the document, and while this letter would seem to be the draft in question, there is no means by which the point can be settled.

Beauharnois's letter of October 6 refers to another source of information on La Vérendrye. This second source may have been the only information available to him at the time: the document, summarized by Beauharnois, was a letter to the governor from the Jesuit Father Pierre du Jaunay, written from his mission at Michilimackinac on July 11. This letter—no longer extant—mentioned the Mantannes and the prospects of successful mission efforts among them. It stated that there were seven villages of these people, the smallest of which contained fifteen hundred souls; that according to reports, the people called the Pananas were still more numerous; and that just beyond them were the Pananis. It is difficult to believe that if Beauharnois had received by early October the detailed account of the expedition of 1738–39, he should have depended on a second-hand authority rather than on the explorer's own record. One is forced to conclude that the communication of May 28 from La Vérendrye had been very brief, was not the original detailed account now sought, and that Beauharnois had not, even by October, seen such a narrative.

Beauharnois's dispatch to Paris on October 6 was accompanied by an extract from a journal of La Vérendrye. This might be the record sought, but no such item is preserved in

Paris. There is, however, an extract of another journal in the archives in Paris which contains information on the customs of the Mantannes as well as reports about the Spanish.[4] The information in it was taken from the reports of the two men La Vérendrye had left on the Missouri at his departure for Fort La Reine in December 1738. These two men are said to have returned to Fort La Reine on September 29, 1739. Beauharnois, in Quebec, could of course not have known of this event by October 6.

There is therefore no way in which to establish the time at which Beauharnois received from La Vérendrye a detailed account of his activities from July 1738 to May 1739. Nor can we establish that the governor ever received such an account. We do know that the explorer visited the governor in August 1740. The visit would have afforded the officer and the governor every opportunity to discuss the information obtained in 1738 and 1739.

In any case, there is no evidence that a draft of the journal of 1738–39 describing the first journey to the country of the Mantannes was ever forwarded to Paris. Nor is there any suggestion in the surviving documents that Beauharnois ever received this record. There is, in short, no way to fix precisely the terminal date for the composition of this important document.

The lack of a closing signature or of any endorsements of sender or recipient seems to be enough proof that the draft is not from official or personal papers of Beauharnois. The manuscript is a signature of sheets sewed together, and looks very much as though it had been taken from a bound volume. It is possible that it is a copybook draft, made from an original in the absence of the author. It was not corrected by La Vérendrye, and a number of mistakes and omissions that might have been corrected by him still remain.

Examination of the paper and ink of the manuscript affords no light as to the precise date of the draft. The paper appears to be of the period to which the contents relate. It is handmade laid paper, and several sheets show a dim watermark, a fleur-de-lis with letters or numerals. The manuscript, in other words, gives every evidence of being a contemporary copy; it does not appear to be a copy made at a later date by, say, a student of La Vérendrye.

This document has been discussed at length because of the incautious use to which it has been put by some scholars, who persist in referring to it as a journal, without qualification. Since the document is a draft, rather than a letter actually received, it is scarcely the primary evidence it has almost universally been considered. On the other hand, despite doubts concerning certain points in it and the risk of placing too much weight on any particular detail, the account as a whole is convincing and gives every evidence of general truthfulness and reliability. Even casual statements, such as those on minor incidents of travel and those on customs of the native people, could only have been made by an eyewitness.

In composing the original letter, the author, un-questionably La Vérendrye, surely had beside him his actual field journals for reference. These must have been more detailed and complete at certain points and less so at others than the present draft. Study reveals that it includes material that would not have appeared in the field journals and was interpolated, while other details that would have been in the field notes must have been omitted. Since the letter was being written for a superior and was more than an account of mere dates and events, trivial details that might be of value to historians were probably deleted. Other remarks were inserted to clarify or extend the original notes and furnish additional information. La Vérendrye would report only such matters as he thought would interest his superiors, and would emphasize such material as would enable him to continue his western explorations.[5] Surely, also, unrecognizable errors must have crept into the text.

It is therefore not wise to place implicit faith in specific details of this record that are not verifiable by other means. Nor is it wise to assume, as some have done, that the document is a flawless record of the accomplishments of the command during this period. Yet precise conclusions have been based on this document.

Before examining more closely the contents of this record of La Vérendrye's journey, we should review his knowledge of the region he was about to penetrate and his objectives in making the expedition. For several years before his departure from Fort La Reine in the fall of 1738, La Vérendrye had had reasonably accurate information from native sources about the region and its inhabitants. From Crees and Assiniboins, and even from members of the sedentary western tribes themselves, he had heard of the character of the peoples he could expect to, meet and had even been told of whites who occupied the lower reaches of the great River of the West.

Of the great western stream itself, La Vérendrye soon learned that it did not flow out of Lake Winnipeg, as he had at first been led to expect, but that it was part of a separate drainage system. That he should have been unaware of the relationship between the Missouri and the Mississippi, whose headwaters were in part known, is no cause for surprise. Information of this sort could only have been available in the Illinois country—and La Vérendrye never went in that direction.

La Vérendrye had previously believed that the great stream he was seeking flowed to the west and hence must connect with a Sea of the West. By 1737, however, he had come to think that its general course was to the south and hence (as was then conceived) into the Pacific Ocean. This reorientation of the geographical problem was of considerable importance to him. Such a western river, if it flowed into the Pacific, could only lead toward Spanish settlements, and exploration in that quarter was no part of his plans, any more than toward Hudson Bay. Here is another clue to the apparent lack of interest on the part of the La Vérendryes in trade southwestward from Fort La Reine. The father and his party in 1738 pushed in that direction because he was obliged to do so. His two sons, four years later, went much farther to the south and west, but there is no evidence that they carried on a vigorous trade in that direction at any time. These visits must soon have shown that trade with the village peoples of the upper Missouri was unlikely to produce beaver of a quality comparable to that from more northerly regions. The difficulties of transporting those they did obtain must also have loomed large in their thinking. And if southwestern exploration led but to the Spanish, the interest of traders would certainly cool. Yet such knowledge as this could

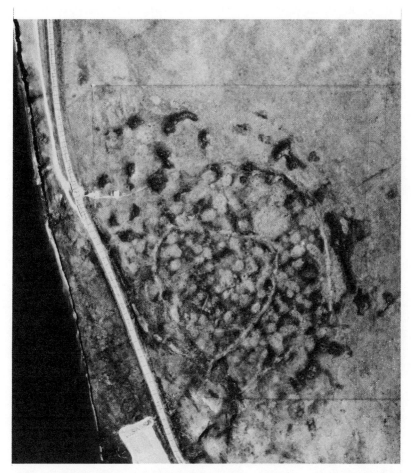

Fig. 3. Aerial photograph of the Double Ditch Site. This fortified Mandan village is on the east bank of the Missouri River nine miles north of Bismarck, North Dakota. The light-colored circles are earth lodge locations; the two ditches that give the site its name are clearly marked. The village is a State Historic Site, under the supervision of the State Historical Society of North Dakota. (Photograph courtesy of the North Dakota State Highway Department.)

scarcely be discussed in communications intended for the ear of the colonial minister and is quite lacking in documents of the period.

It is not surprising that La Vérendrye's informants were not always consistent in their accounts of minor details about the westerners and their country. But there was a general truthfulness in their reports, based on actual contacts in trade and in war, which the French discovered during their visits. They had been told of sedentary, gardening peoples who lived in dwellings made of earth and in fortified villages scattered along an important western stream—so unlike the shifting camps of the peoples of the woodland—and that is precisely what La Vérendrye found when he reached the upper Missouri River (see, for example, figure 3).

His informants made no false claims about the source of their knowledge of this region. They first spoke of their relations with these western peoples as having taken the form of military raids and child stealing—claims which have an undeniably authentic ring. But this hostile relationship seemed to alternate with yet another: that of formal trade, seasonal in nature. This alternating pattern of trading and raiding seems to have been an old one, with roots deep in the prehistoric past.[6]

The Crees and Monsonis, like the Assiniboins, through La Vérendrye's own trade with them, had for a number of years been able to play the part of middlemen in trade between the French and more distant peoples. The interdependence between the Crees and Assiniboins on the one hand and the village dwellers on the other is clearly witnessed by the account of their trade. The new peoples welcomed the visits of the French. The Assiniboins, on the other hand, who were the actual agents of the contact of the French with the Missouri River peoples, probably tried to delay advance in that direction, for if the French were to penetrate to the Missouri and establish themselves there in regular trade, Assiniboin interests would surely suffer. They probably knowingly contributed the varying counsel given the commandant about the western Indians, bearded white persons, the Spanish, and other matters.

What then can be said of La Vérendrye's immediate purposes in pushing beyond Fort La Reine in the fall of 1738?

From the outset, when he first took command of the Posts of the North more than ten years earlier, his duty to explore, and especially to discover a route to the Sea of the West, had been uppermost in importance, at least to the court. And progress in that direction, though frequently delayed, had nevertheless been made. A chain of posts now extended from Kamanistikwia to the Assiniboine River, all of them established and maintained by La Vérendrye's group. By any count this was a remarkable achievement. But the unknown had to be entered once more, and time was short. When La Vérendrye visited the East in 1737, Beauharnois had been forced to warn him that this was his last opportunity to fulfill the conditions of his commission. Beauharnois could only say that if he did not succeed, it would be necessary to replace him. No longer could La Vérendrye put off his journey to the Sea of the West.

There is scant hint in surviving documents of plans and preparations for travel southwestward from Fort La Reine. It cannot be doubted that La Vérendrye was now well aware of the important differences such travel would make in his arrangements. By the time he reached Fort La Reine, he must have well understood the real character of such long overland journeys. Accustomed to water transport and moving men and goods and packs of furs over vast distances, he must still have hesitated over the new overland expedition.

Among the articles La Vérendrye issued to the men who were to accompany him, according to the document, were shoes *(souliers)*. The fur traders were accustomed to wearing moccasins, the only footgear suited to the fragile birchbark canoe of the trade. The soft-soled moccasins of the Indians of the Great Lakes region had been adopted by the very first settlers of New France. Whether the shoes La Vérendrye issued were leather ones of European origin, and which might have been brought from the East for the purpose, or the hard-soled moccasins used by such Indians of the plains as the Assiniboins, from whom they could have been obtained, the specific reference to footgear is direct evidence that La Vérendrye and his men were prepared for an ordeal of a new sort.

It is surprising that the long and trying journey to the River of the West should have been undertaken in October, so late in the season, though La Vérendrye seems at first to have intended to winter in the country of the Mantannes. The Indians perhaps minimized the hardships of the journey, and La Vérendrye later implied that it should have been possible to make the round trip in no more than thirty-two to forty days' traveling time. We have little evidence of other details about which he must have inquired, and of which he was no doubt informed. He was soon to become aware of the character of the grassland prairies, where the lack of firewood could be remedied by using *bois de vache* (buffalo chips); of the often great distances between sources of water; of the movements of game such as buffalo according to the season and the weather; and the like. Not only was the party guided by the Indians from Fort La Reine, but from that point on they were completely dependent on them, even for their food. En route to the Missouri, the Assiniboins were following the buffalo in their fall hunt, according to ancient custom, and the French leader warned his men to carry as much food as they could. No longer could they count on supplies carried in canoes or stored in caches; now their only commissary was on their backs, or on the dog travois of the Indians, and this in addition to other necessary equipment.

For a variety of reasons it is difficult to establish La Vérendrye's route precisely from the document. The routine day-to-day events of the trip must have been of concern at the time, but it is hardly surprising that they were not included in an official letter. It is also understandable that such geographic information as is mentioned, and which might be of help in retracing the route of the party, is referred to in the most casual manner. The recipient of the letter would scarcely be interested in the precise location or a description of such minor landmarks as the "first mountain" or the second, and nothing has survived that makes the identification of such landmarks more than reasonable guesses, taking into account all remarks on direction, distance, and speed. But even the latter are matters for speculation, since we do not know the means by which each was judged. Certain assumptions that may help one understand other direct statements are of course possible. There is reason to believe that the party had with it instruments for making careful observations, including the compass, astrolabe, and pocket watch. We may assume, for example, from the reference to a compass direction during the son's visit to the second Mantanne village that this instrument was the authority for statements of direction. An astrolabe would have permitted the observation of latitude taken at the first Mantanne village, presumably using the North Star. But even if the party used such instruments from time to time, we need to know more than we do of the quality of the instruments themselves, not to mention the skill of those using them and the accuracy of the record that has been preserved.

There are also problems concerning statements about distance and rate of travel, particularly since the explorers were in an area and under circumstances new to them—and their statements, such as they are, are subject to verification only in small measure. Their route was largely at the discretion of their Indian guides, whose purposes differed from those of the French. The trip was furthermore made on foot, with a mixed party including women and children, dog travois, and the like. Competence in judging such matters as the rate of travel and estimates of distance by men unaccustomed to such travel may well be questioned. But here, as elsewhere, means of verifying the statements are lacking, and the document must be accepted or rejected as it stands.

It is possible to check the account against present-day knowledge when references are made to topographic or to such prominent cultural features as the fortified villages of the Mantannes. Unfortunately, these features are problematical: topographic features are sometimes given no more than casual mention, and the identification of the fortified villages is a special problem, involving ethnographic, archeological, and linguistic considerations.

The statements of the record of 1738 and 1739, therefore, must be reviewed in the light of what has since become known of the area they visited. This is a major objective of the present book, with the purpose of tracing as closely as possible the route followed and identifying as precisely as practical the places they reached. The judgments that have been made by historians and ethnographers are generally accurate, but some conclusions have been reached that are not acceptable when the evidence available today is considered, and must be rejected.

Leaving Fort La Reine on October 18, 1738, the party reached, on the third day, a point estimated as being twenty-six leagues from the fort, by proceeding south by west. If the league is understood as representing three miles, the distance covered would be a little more than seventy-five miles, a very good speed for a mixed party afoot and engaged in hunting.[7] Using La Vérendrye's sixteen- to twenty-day estimate, we infer that a good rate of travel for a party on foot would have been six leagues, or about eighteen miles a day—not quite the distance suggested by the figure of twenty-six leagues. Some historians (among them Orin G. Libby) have greatly overestimated the party's speed, probably because they simply forgot to take into account the fact that the party was on foot.

Since the party consisted of nearly half Assiniboins, their course was, furthermore, not as direct as it might have been had the French been able to go directly to their objective. The route was frequently deflected from a direct one by the necessity of obtaining food, fuel, and water. The document therefore preserves accounts of hunting buffalo, which were found in great numbers in the plains of what is now southwestern Manitoba.

The journal of 1738 was a traverse, and the region lacked prominent geographical features or reference points by which such a journey might be corrected or adjusted from time to time. There is no evidence that during the trip a map was being made, which would have required taking frequent observations and would permit criticism and revision, either at the time or now. Although we do not know that a map was not actually made, it seems unlikely that anything more than the simplest record of estimated distance and direction was recorded in the field journals. The journey must have seemed at times to the

French like an ocean voyage, with little beside the sun and stars for useful reference points.

A more delicate problem is that of reckoning the direction of travel. Russell Reid has examined the matter of magnetic declination in 1738, assuming that recorded directions were based on the compass. He has shown that correction for declination is necessary to adjust recorded courses to modern maps.[8] Yet previous studies of the route of the expedition have never taken this fundamental matter into account.

Related to the problem of the declination of the compass needle is that of properly interpreting the named compass points according to the wind rose, or the compass card used by the French. The fact that there are significant differences between the French and English names for compass points has likewise been overlooked. Thus, the rendering of the first course given, *sud quard* (i.e., *quart*) *de sudouest*, as "south by southwest," as has been done, is quite erroneous.[9] The French term means, literally, "south one point southwest" or, as we would say today, "south by west." This error on the part of some translators makes a difference of eleven and one-quarter degrees in computations.[10] Other errors of this kind appear in all the other published translations of the document.

In addition to delays and variations from the intended course arising from the buffalo hunt, from the mixed character of the party, and from other factors, there is still another source of delay and variation. On the third day of the trip a group of forty Assiniboin families overtook them, desiring a council. This was but one of several such incidents affecting the journey. This particular band did not follow the French party, but remained near Fort La Reine. Time was nevertheless lost. Later it became necessary to make a wide detour to visit an even larger encampment.

The party came to the "first mountain" at a distance of some seventy-five miles (twenty-six leagues) from their point of departure. There is only one natural feature in such a radius that could qualify as the elevation intended: the Pembina Mountain,[11] although other points have been suggested. Libby, for instance, suggested that it may have been Star Mound, near

Snowflake, Manitoba, but Reid has shown that such localized geographic features can scarcely be identified with conviction.[12]

Pembina Mountain, however, is not a localized natural feature that can provide precision in reference. It is, in fact, a "mountain" only in local usage. Its technical name, the Pembina Escarpment, more accurately describes this feature, which is as much as eighty miles long.

It would obviously be unwarranted to pinpoint on a modern map a specific turning point as the landmark intended in the journal, since this escarpment was in the region the party crossed. A number of conspicuous hills, often referred to as mountains or mounds—the latter term stemming from the fact there were often burial mounds on them—are possible candidates for the landmark. Among these are Star Mound (or Nebogwawin Butte), Calf Mountain, Medicine or Signal Hill, and Pilot Mound Hill.[13] The first two of these have been suggested as being the "first mountain." Star Mound, an inconspicuous feature with local relief of only fifty feet, was believed to be the "first mountain" by Libby. The other feature is Calf Mountain, a small hill rising slightly above the surrounding prairie southwest of the present town of Darlingford, Manitoba. Calf Mountain was the site of an Indian mound originally about ten feet high.[14]

Calf Mountain appears to have some cultural significance bearing on the problem of identifying La Vérendrye's "first mountain." Human and buffalo bones were found in early excavations at Calf Mountain. Its name itself is perhaps a translation of a native name, referring to the burial of both human and animal remains.[15] Other artificial mounds, containing associated human and buffalo burials, have been excavated by archeologists along the valleys of the Red, Pembina, Souris, Sheyenne, and Missouri rivers, in both Canada and present North Dakota.[16] Places such as Calf Mountain may have been occasional stopping places, perhaps for ceremonial purposes. Such a stop may even have been made in 1738, although unrecorded.

There are two other major features in the area worthy of note, although they have not been suggested as a La Vérendrye

Fig. 4. Prairie in north-central North Dakota, not far from where La Vérendrye commented on the "magnificent plains." (Photograph by W. R. Wood.)

landmark. Medicine Hill or Signal Hill is a large hill northwest of Pelican Lake in the Pembina River valley. It is on the crest of one of the highest elevations in the Tiger Hills country, and is the location of large burial mounds.[17] Pilot Mound Hill, or Pilot Mound, as it is commonly known, is also a well-known local landmark from which an extensive view of the surrounding Manitoba plain can be seen.

Although the matter has hardly been resolved, we agree that "first mountain" referred not to a small and localized elevation, but most likely to Pembina Mountain. The estimated distance from this "first mountain" to the second one in the record of 1738 was twenty-four leagues; the direction, west by north. This distance and direction lead only to Turtle Mountain, another geographic feature of this region not unlike Pembina Mountain in being an extensive upland lacking real landmarks. Turtle Mountain provides a more commanding view in that it has a local relief of about seven hundred feet above the surrounding plain. This forested upland, surrounded by grassland, received its name from the Indians, who saw the uplift area as being turtle-shaped. Those familiar with the terrain agree that this upland was probably the elevation referred to in the record as the "second mountain."[18]

The party had now crossed part of the western basin of the Red River and had climbed perhaps one thousand feet in elevation. Their course had been erratic, for we read that in order to go two or three leagues in a straight line the party actually had to travel three or four. The march was fatiguing because of the constant necessity for climbing and descending hills and valleys many times daily. They comment on the "magnificent plains" three to four leagues in extent that they crossed on the way (fig. 4).

The route is described even less precisely after leaving the "second mountain." Having already been delayed by the lengthening of the trip and several stops, the party finally went as much as twenty-two leagues out of their way to visit a large encampment of Assiniboins. There are no clues as to the location of this camp, but some would have it that the detour was toward the west and that the distance recorded would have taken the party west across the loop of the Souris (Mouse)

River.[19] There is, however, no evidence of the direction taken on this detour. There is, in fact, no mention of any stream or valley, such as that of the Souris, or of any other body of water they crossed between the Assiniboine and the Missouri rivers. In view of the fact that it was now late October and the season was a dry one, they may have followed the course of the Souris River, even though the stream is not mentioned. The opinion that they reached the far side of the Souris River loop is, however, pure speculation.

Having spent parts of two days at the large Assiniboin camp, they once more got underway, proceeding to a rendezvous with a party from the Mantannes. The Assiniboins had anticipated the approach to the Missouri by sending scouts ahead to arrange for such a meeting. From the large Assiniboin camp to this point required parts of eight days' travel to cover only seventeen leagues. If this distance is correct, one explanation for the slower pace may be the fact that the party was now enlarged by the addition of more than a hundred Indian families.

The final leg of the journey seems to have been covered with better speed after the rendezvous with the emissaries from the Mantannes. Again the composition of the camp changed, and only the best walkers continued. By the evening of the third day of this march from the rendezvous, the party reached a point some seven leagues from the first of the Mantanne fortified villages. They had crossed a region later to be called the Coteau des Prairies (prairie highlands) and had entered the basin of the Missouri River.

The account now becomes detailed in describing the strange new peoples in the neighborhood of the great western river. Observations of these peoples and their customs are often quite specific, in spite of the brevity of the party's visit. It is not necessary here to examine the observations closely, for analysis has established the authentic character of this first account of these horticultural earth lodge dwellers of the upper Missouri River, although a few minor details can be questioned.[20] There is general concurrence on the ethnographic details, but a number of problems have been raised that must be treated in detail. The most important of these is the issue raised by Libby concerning the identification of the people La Vérendrye called the Mantannes.

From the time historians first became aware of the achievements of the La Vérendryes in reaching the upper Missouri, it was assumed that the people called the Mantannes (singular: Mantanne) were none other than the Mandan Indians. The first modern account of this expedition, by Pierre Margry, identified these people as the Mandans, and most historians have accepted his conclusion, which seems the obvious one.[21] Libby, however, challenged the identification, asserting that it was "extremely doubtful whether La Vérendrye ever saw the Mandans or came within a day's journey of them."[22] To anticipate a conclusion, however, the data and later scholarship flatly do not support Libby's contention, the essence of which follows.

Among other things, Libby asserted that the description of the first of the Mantanne villages visited by La Vérendrye "is clear evidence of its non-Mandan character."[23] This statement is based on several observations, including the fact that there is no mention in the account of the central open plaza of the Mandan villages, with its distinctive barrel-like *och-ta* (sacred "canoe") and ceremonial lodge. On the contrary, the record states that all the streets, "squares," and huts resembled each other.[24]

Libby laid great stress on the distinctions—as he knew them—between Mandan and Hidatsa villages. Surveys of existing Hidatsa archeological sites at the time, as well as most of the historic accounts, seemed to agree that Hidatsa villages were without order, or anything that La Vérendrye might have referred to as streets or open places. Mandan villages, on the other hand, seemed consistently to have at least one large open space, with a ceremonial lodge, slightly different from other houses in the village, forming part of the circle of dwellings around this open area. Libby asserted that La Vérendrye could not have failed to see and report this ceremonial lodge, had he actually visited a Mandan village. Yet later visitors, among them Alexander Henry and Lewis and Clark, likewise fail to give an account of such a feature.[25] The omission of a reference to the ceremonial lodge, then, does not mean that La Vérendrye did not see such a feature; mention of corn- and meat-drying scaffolds, as well as scaffolds for the disposal of the dead outside the village, were equally conspicuous in all historical earth lodge villages, and no note is made of them. The lack of mention of the Mandan ceremonial center in the Mantanne village is, therefore, not as significant as Libby made it out to be.

In a later article Libby revealed that much of the authority for his hypothesis had been derived from traditions of "native tribes actually living in the west, whose knowledge of their local geography and tribal life for the eighteenth century is as complete and exact as ours is vague and unscientific."[26] This value judgment on his part set the tone for all of his efforts in the matter. He preferred to rely on modern native tradition for evidence in preference to any other source. The choice, of course, is a personal one, but there has been little acceptance of Libby's conclusion by those intimately acquainted with Missouri River Indian cultures.

The Hidatsas, he said, had a "distinct tradition of southward migration" from some point in Canada or north-central North Dakota, coming from that region to the Missouri, which they crossed and joined the Mandans. Libby claimed to have obtained information from the Hidatsas of the Fort Berthold Indian Reservation on the "exact location of this crossing." Both the Mandans and Hidatsas, he said, spoke of the event "as a matter of common knowledge." It is scarcely necessary to point out that the acceptance of oral tradition of informants of the early twentieth century concerning matters which took place nearly two centuries earlier is naive and historically unsound. Several specific claims based on such sources by Libby have been denied by competent scholars.[27]

Evidence contradicting Libby's Hidatsa hypothesis is convincing. To begin with, Will has shown that there is every reason to believe that the Mantannes were the historic Mandans. The word *Mandan* is clearly of Siouan origin, rather than Algonquian, as Libby supposed. One Sioux name for them is *Mawatana* and another is *Mawatadani*, and the Omahas (another Siouan-speaking plains group) called them the *Mawa' dani*.[28] There is no evidence that this term was ever applied to the Hidatsas, and a concordance of native terms from early documents would probably demonstrate that the French form *Mantanne* is the exact equivalent of the English *Mandan.*

Libby's Hidatsa hypothesis also entailed the identity of the two Indian groups La Vérendrye noted as living down the Missouri, the Panaux (or Pananas) and the Pananis. This he did by identifying them with the Mandans and Arikaras, respectively. His identification was at once contradicted.[29] As Will aptly noted, "To those who can readily see that 'Panani' is not Pawnee, that 'des Missouris' is not the Missouri, it may appear clear that 'Mantannes' are not Mandan and that 'Panana' are Mandan—but it might also be contended under the same theory that 'Assinipoels' could not be Assiniboin."[30]

Libby believed that the earth lodge village visited by La Vérendrye was in the vicinity of the Little Knife River, on the basis of the observation of latitude taken by the son at that village, and which is recorded as forty-eight degrees and twelve minutes. No other direct evidence supports the Hidatsas as having lived in this location at the time—or at any other time. The recorded figures may have been carelessly transcribed in the manuscript, or the instrument—presumably an astrolabe—may not have been accurate or properly read.[31] It would therefore be unwise to accept the recorded observation as precise and final evidence. Libby goes so far as to say that those who refuse to accept the observation fail to explain why La Vérendrye "could not perform the relatively simple task of ascertaining the correct latitude."[32] His remark is startlingly naive.

Other students have commented on the difficulty of accepting this observation of latitude. Warren Upham—himself a competent surveyor—remarked that the observation or the record "was most surely erroneous, exceeding the true latitude by nearly one degree," and had no difficulty in making such a correction. Other historians familiar with the ground, such as Charles E. DeLand and Doane Robinson, also assume that the Mantannes were in the Heart River region, thus, by implication, rejecting the recorded observation.[33]

Archeological field work in North Dakota, furthermore, provides no support for Libby's hypothesis. A great deal of such work was carried out by the State Historical Society of North Dakota and by the Smithsonian Institution before Garrison Dam was built and before most of the area in North Dakota upstream from the mouth of the Knife River was flooded by Lake Sakakawea. A large number of archeological sites were recorded above Garrison Dam, but only a few of them are relevant to our problem. Most such sites are prehistoric campsites or burial mounds; earth lodge villages are noted for their rarity, particularly since they are so common below the mouth of the Knife River, near Stanton. Most of these villages were occupied by refugee groups of Mandans, Hidatsas, and Arikaras many decades after the time of La Vérendrye's visit.[34]

One curious site, north of Lake Sakakawea, which was investigated by Thad. Hecker in 1938, has a number of features that necessitate brief mention here. This site, on the White Earth River several miles north of the Missouri valley and called the White Earth Creek site, consisted of a fortified enclosure of about 1.2 acres. There were no surface indications of houses within the curving fortification ditch, which was reinforced by four bastions and a line of palisade posts within the ditch. The artifacts from the site have not yet been described, so it is impossible to comment on the identity of its builders except to say that it may be prehistoric, since no Euro-American trade goods seem to have been found.[35]

Several features invite its comparison with the first Mantanne fort: (1) the fact that it is several miles from the Missouri River, (2) it is on a hill and fortified by a ditch, and (3) the fortifications are augmented by four bastions. Since, however, the fortified area is only 1.2 acres and contained no evidence for dwellings such as characterize villages along the Missouri River, the comparison with the village of 130 houses of the first Mantanne fort is not especially convincing, especially in view of its location so far from the mouth of the Heart River.

In any case, the mouth of the Knife River, near Stanton, marks the northwesternmost effective limit for native village cultures along the Missouri River before they were disturbed by white contact. Garrison Reservoir has in fact been referred to as "the northern periphery of the Upper Missouri culture area."[36] It is therefore very unlikely that any support for Libby's hypothesis will be found in this area in the future, for the requisite villages neighboring the Mantanne fort simply are not to be found there.

Libby located the first Mantanne village west of the Souris or Mouse River. We have already seen that such a location is not supported by any reliable evidence, but the assertion was necessary for his hypothesis. We can only be sure that the first Mantanne village was within a day's march of the second, on the Missouri River, from the fact that the party consisting of the Chevalier, the Sieur Nolan, and some *engagés* and Indians needed only parts of two days to complete the trip.[37]

Libby concluded that the party had reached the site of a "very large and very old Hidatsa winter village" about thirty miles south of latitude forty-eight degrees and twelve minutes and near the mouth of Shell Creek, on the north side of the Missouri.[38] He later abandoned this locality in favor of another site even farther up the Missouri, which he called "Old Crossing."

Roland B. Dixon was unable to accept the suggestion that the earth lodge peoples visited by La Vérendrye lived so far from the traditional Heart River location and noted that to accept the northerly location for either a Mandan or a Hidatsa village conflicted with "accessible evidence and tradition."[39]

In 1916, in a reiteration of his hypothesis, Libby announced the identification of a new site as that of the village on the Missouri River visited by La Vérendrye's son in 1738.[40] This site, he said, was that of an old Hidatsa village on the east bank of the Missouri River, in present McLean County, one mile south of the mouth of the Little Knife River and more than 180 miles above Bismarck. The site had, unfortunately, "washed into the river," but it was "well known locally." The old garden and burial places, he said, could still be pointed out. The locality, according to his claims, was known as Old Crossing; the Hidatsas had first crossed the Missouri River there. It is not necessary to examine in detail the basis for his claims that this lost site was that of the village of 1738: they have already been examined and rejected by Will. It is worth noting that the name

Old Crossing does not appear in historical literature before 1916, when it was first used by Libby.[41]

Libby's claim of positive identification of the long-sought site of 1738 was never documented. There is no hint, for example, that he had found the necessary number of associated earth lodge village sites nearby. Libby and his assistant, Herbert C. Fish, searched in vain for surviving sites in the region. Any identification, of course, requires the discovery of not just one site, but of a group of villages. Whereas one could believe the partial or total loss of one (or of several) sites to the Missouri River, the loss of all of them strains belief.[42] Furthermore, the smaller first village, away from the river, has not been found. In view of the documentation and its rejection by serious and competent local scholars intimately familiar with the archeology of the area, it is curious that some general works of wide circulation still accept the Libby hypothesis.[43]

Another archeological site, near Bismarck, must now be considered as a possible location for the first Mantanne village. This site is on Apple Creek, a small tributary of the Missouri which flows into that stream from the east and a little below the mouth of the Heart River.[44] The village, discovered by Walter D. Powell in 1936, was acquired by the state of North Dakota and was established on February 1, 1937, as Menoken Indian Village State Park, under the supervision of the State Historical Society. The park is on the south bank of the creek some twelve miles east of Bismarck. It was named for the neighboring community of Menoken; the name is not of Indian origin.

Personnel from the State Historical Society of North Dakota, among others, have studied this site and data from it for its relevance to the La Vérendrye expedition in 1738.[45] The village is distinctive in being located away from the Missouri River, east of that stream, yet within a "day's journey" of the historic Mandan earth lodge villages near the mouth of the Heart River. Menoken is on a terrace above the heavily wooded creek bottoms, and affords a clear view across the bottomlands toward the north and northeast and of several buttelike elevations back from the creek, well in accordance with the account of the first Mantanne fort. Remains of a ditch surrounding the village away from the creek bank, and

Fig. 5. The Menoken Site, on Apple Creek, about twelve miles east of Bismarck, North Dakota. The fortification ditch, bastions, and house sites are not very distinct at this village. Menoken is a State Historic Site, under the supervision of the State Historical Society of North Dakota. (Photograph by W. R. Wood.)

paralleled by an interior earthwork preserving the remains of four large bastions, are still visible (fig. 5).

Excavators at Menoken in 1938 explored the ditch and interior earthwork and provided some information on dwellings through the clearing of one of the lodge sites. The chief excavator, Thad. Hecker, was of the opinion that it was a village of the historic Mandans of an age appropriate to have been visited by La Vérendrye. He went on to point out that the only region in which numerous earth lodge villages of the appropriate age have been found was at the mouth of the Heart River, which is within the distance from Menoken required by the account of 1738.[46]

Local students, like George Will and Thad. Hecker, agree that the Menoken site is in an appropriate location with respect to the Heart River villages of the Mandans, and that there is as yet no other candidate in the area for the first Mantanne village. Furthermore, the necessary earth lodge villages simply do not exist in the vicinity of "Old Crossing," so there is clearly consensus that La Vérendrye visited the vicinity of the mouth of the Heart River.

Nevertheless, Menoken's case is far from secure. Like the first Mantanne village, it is fortified, the defenses having bastions, and it is in an appropriate location—a prairie setting. There are, however, a number of discrepancies that cast doubt on its identity as the village of 1738. First, it is far too small to be reliably identified as the village of 130 houses that La Vérendrye visited. Since the fortified part of the site contains only three acres, there is no possibility that this number of houses could have been built in the fortified area, even given the possibility that part of the site has been removed by erosion. Some of the houses at Menoken are outside the ditch, but even so, the site scarcely approaches the magnitude of the one described by La Vérendrye. There are still other features at Menoken that do not agree with the 1738 village description: for example, the ditch at Menoken is only five feet deep, not fifteen; and Hecker found no cache pits during his work there, whereas La Vérendrye commented on their large numbers in the village he visited.

Most local students familiar with the problem would

probably agree with the conclusions, as we do, of James E. Sperry, superintendent of the State Historical Society of North Dakota. He feels "not only that there is too little information from excavation of the site to identify it properly, but also that existing archaeological survey coverage away from the main stream is inadequate to allow reasonable discussion of potential sites." Contrary to the opinion of Will and Hecker, Sperry's inspection of the material from the site suggests that it is too early to have been visited by La Vérendrye. In short, the site's identity as the first Mantanne village is not supported by the cursory archeological work that has been done at the site to date. In fact, Sperry suspects that "the blanket of cultural material over and well outside the fortification ditch represents a somewhat different and later occupation." He concludes that the case for Menoken is open, but that its identification as the one La Vérendrye visited is not justified by the available archeological data, even though he believes that La Vérendrye's journey carried him to some point not far from the mouth of the Heart River.[47]

Although the probability that Menoken is the first Mantanne village is not very good, it is obvious that the valley of Apple Creek deserves far more attention than it has had to date. There is traditional and documentary evidence that the Mandans built villages near the mouth of the stream, but the rest of its course is all but unknown to archeologists.[48]

La Vérendrye seems to have made no extravagant claims of discoveries during his journey in 1738 and 1739, nor did he pretend to knowledge that he did not possess. It is true that his letter concludes with the statement that he had discovered (as he believed) a river flowing toward the west. Unlike other streams of which he was aware, it did not drain toward Hudson Bay. But he merely said that he would obtain more complete information on it.

In spite of the problems raised by his account, it must be regarded as a restrained and essentially truthful record of observations he actually made in the field, remarkably un-cluttered with inferences based on those observations. There is an element of surprise in the record of what he saw at the first Mantanne village; it is probably because the fortifications, which he had never seen before, and the houses and customs of the Mantannes were new and strange to him. Nowhere in his account, however, is there any hint that he exaggerated or intentionally misrepresented any of the novel things he saw among these people.

His achievement in reaching the Missouri River, a goal the La Vérendryes had been seeking for more than a decade, is passed over with scarcely a comment. It seems certain that he now realized that the Missouri, important as it was, would not lead them to a Sea of the West. And in reporting to his superiors, it would not do to imply that he had failed: La Vérendrye did not claim the discovery of the long-sought waterway, for now he knew better.

He concluded his account with reserve. He could probably imagine the frowns that would cross certain faces, but he could not claim what he did not believe. It was unlikely that even Maurepas would appreciate the great step in geographical knowledge that had been taken under his direction and that reflected great credit on the throne of Louis XV. The western commandant, however well he understood the importance of what he had done, could scarcely make such persons un-derstand. There was tragic irony in his predicament.

His disillusionment was heightened by the lack of furs on the plains. In penetrating to the Missouri valley, La Vérendrye had passed well beyond the margin of the eastern woodlands. Beaver and other fur bearers were, of course, to be found on the plains and along its watercourses, but their numbers were smaller than along the lakes and streams to the east. Con-versely, on the prairies the buffalo, probably no more than rare strays in the woodlands, took the place in native economy of the smaller fur bearers elsewhere. The dependence of the Assiniboins on the buffalo, as shown in La Vérendrye's account and in so many others, also characterized the economies of the village-dwelling Mandans, Hidatsas, and Arikaras, in spite of their heavy reliance on their gardens. In any event, the role of the smaller fur bearers in the northern plains was clearly a minor one.

These facts have a bearing on the policies and acts of La Vérendrye in the years after 1739. The Assiniboins and Crees had disappointed him with their lack of concern over supplying the pelts needed in the trade. It seems likely that La Vérendrye did not immediately comprehend the full significance of the dependence of the Assiniboins on the buffalo. Once out on the prairies with them, on the long trek to the Missouri, he must have been led to a much clearer understanding of the fact that many fewer pelts were available in this new setting.

It is not hard to believe that La Vérendrye was disappointed and half-hearted about pursuing the explorations of 1738–39. It is true that his sons returned to the region and even went far beyond the Missouri, but the father did not. He must have foreseen the impossibility of trade, at least of the kind he knew and sought, in that direction. The establishment of posts, or at least of profitable trade in return for pelts, was the sole means by which the old search for a Sea of the West could be maintained, since the king himself would provide no other. Is it to be wondered that La Vérendrye seems himself to have been satisfied with but one visit to the mighty Missouri, or that almost at once he turned his eyes in other directions—toward the valley of the Saskatchewan, for example, a likelier prospect for the "better beaver" of the North?

5
The Years 1739–42

THE Missouri River—the mysterious River of the West—had at last been reached (fig. 6). More than seven years had elapsed since the summer of 1731, when the first steps were taken in this direction, steps that were frequently difficult, sometimes dangerous, and in one instance tragic. Yet the accomplishments of those years could not have been properly evaluated at Versailles. Even had the court appreciated the vast distances yet to be covered before a Sea of the West could be reached, it would scarcely have given the explorer due credit for the arduous work he had completed to date.

As for La Vérendrye, one wonders whether even he was aware of how far he yet was from his ultimate objective. It was many leagues from Quebec to the upper Missouri, but as great a distance remained to the Pacific, over regions even more difficult to cross. Did La Vérendrye really appreciate the true character of the geographic problems and the real nature of the assignment he had requested so many years ago? Now he was aware, from first-hand experience, of the character of the prairies and the Great Plains, beyond the familiar woods and waters of the canoe lands. But of private thoughts there is little hint in the documents. Before the governor he spoke with pride

Fig. 6. The Missouri River bottomlands, a few miles north of Bismarck, North Dakota. (Photograph by W. R. Wood.)

of his accomplishments so far rather than of the hazards of the future.

The record of the explorations of 1738 and 1739 concluded with a statement about the River of the West and the fact that it flowed west. La Vérendrye chose to call attention to the possibility of further exploration by water, probably because he had entered a different drainage basin by having crossed the "height of land" of which there had been so frequent mention in earlier maps and documents. He could as yet hardly have foreseen that the true continental divide was of a quite different nature from the almost imperceptible height of land separating waters draining to Hudson Bay from those draining away by way of the River of the West.

Had the ministry cared to weight the accomplishments of La Vérendrye and his assistants fairly, they might have noted that not only had the group established a new base of operations far beyond the Lake of the Woods and explored in a wholly new direction, to the southwest, but they had reached the River of the West itself, an obviously important waterway. They had also begun to probe in other directions. From Fort La Reine, La Vérendrye, in April 1739, had sent his son the Chevalier in the direction of another vast inland lake, to which they were now close, Lake Winnipeg. The Chevalier was to explore it and to discover the streams flowing into it, especially the one called the Rivière Blanche, or the great Saskatchewan.

La Vérendrye seems to have intended to go himself in the direction of Lake Winnipeg when his canoes returned with supplies in the fall. But his plans soon changed, for we find him going then to Michilimackinac instead. The Saskatchewan attracted his attention at this time because of reports of mines in its vicinity. The reports must have been very vague, for the Chevalier was to "make a circuit of the lake." That would of course have taken not weeks, but months. But the real reason for probing in this direction is suggested by the remark that the Chevalier was "to try to prevent the Indians going to the English," by making them hope that La Vérendrye would go to them in person in the near future.

But his affairs took a different turn now, and once more the troublesome matter of finances arose to plague him. When he reached Michilimackinac that summer, his furs were seized. In May of 1738 La Vérendrye had contracted an obligation to the Sieur de Lorme of more than six thousand livres for merchandise for his explorations and commerce. The debt was to be paid in August of 1739 or earlier. But the merchant had misgivings about the loan, for as early as June he obtained permission, which he proceeded to use, to seize the commandant's peltries.[1] This unhappy incident was but one more thorn in his side, one that took some time to resolve. At this point, however, we must turn our attention to other matters affecting La Vérendrye's life.

Two of La Vérendrye's men had been left in the Mantanne village on his departure for Fort La Reine in December 1738. They were to learn the new language and, when their knowledge of it should permit, to gather all possible information on the country. These two men remained among the Mantannes for more than eight months, returning to Fort La Reine in September.[2]

The two Frenchmen had done a conscientious job, and they furnished a great deal of information in addition to that obtained by La Vérendrye during his own brief visit. They found, for example, that at the beginning of June every year, representatives of several nations came to the great villages of the Mantannes on the banks of the Missouri River. These people came on horses to trade with the Mantannes, bringing dressed hides, trimmed and ornamented with feathers and porcupine quills and painted in various colors. They also brought white buffalo robes to trade. From the account it is clear that these visiting tribes were typical plains Indians, now beginning to profit from their possession of horses and, no doubt, firearms. In exchange, the Mantannes traded corn and beans, of which they had an ample supply.

In the spring of 1739, the two men reported, some two hundred families of these visitors arrived, and even more had been present on other occasions. The visitors were from several different tribes. One such people were said to have come from

the direction of the setting sun, where there were said to be
white men who lived in towns and in forts of brick and white
stone. Learning of the presence of Frenchmen among the
Mantannes, the visitors welcomed them. So the French went to
see them, on the opposite side of the Missouri River. In one of
the houses they found a man of great reputation among these
western folk, who spoke the language of the distant white
people. Because the two Frenchmen did not understand the
language—perhaps corrupt Spanish—the visitor used the
language of the Mantannes, telling them that he had been raised
from childhood among the whites. He visited the two Frenchmen several times and seemed quite friendly toward them.

He said that the white persons among whom he had
grown up were very pleasant people, adding that he would be
happy to guide the two to see them, and assuring them that they
would be well received. He had horses to transport them, and it
would be possible to reach their destination before cold weather
set in. It was, however, a great distance, since they would have
to make a great detour to avoid a numerous people, the Gens du
Serpent (People of the Snake). Most of these people, he said,
lived in forts, but the rest were nomadic and occupied a very
large territory. We need not believe that he had very detailed
knowledge of the Gens du Serpent, or indeed that they were in
fact one people. The Frenchmen probably also misunderstood
his reference to their villages as "forts," since only the village
peoples along the Missouri River had fortified villages comparable to those of the Mantannes.

These Gens du Serpent (or Shoshones), we learn, were
enemies of the white people of the West, and were a brave
people, dreaded even by other native tribes. Yet there was no
reason to fear meeting them on the journey to visit the white
people, because a route would be followed to avoid them. The
two Frenchmen, however, declined the man's offer. They had
traded all their goods with the Mantannes and, in any event,
could not undertake such a journey without notifying their
commandant.

The visiting chief gave convincing evidence of the truth of
his claims of having lived among the white peoples to the west.
He described them as white, like the French, and as wearing

beards. They prayed to the "great master of life" in books, which he described as being made of corn leaves. Holding these books, they were accustomed to sing in great houses, where they assembled for prayer. The Frenchmen said that the chief frequently mentioned the names of Jesus and Mary, and he showed them a cross that he had worn around his neck since birth. He described their houses as being made of bricks and receiving light from above—as indeed Spanish missions did.

Of Spanish towns and forts, the chief said that they were surrounded by good walls and wide ditches filled with water, and had drawbridges, gates of iron, and ramparts. The whites used powder, cannon, guns, axes, and knives, the latter of which they traded to the Indians. They grew all kinds of grain, plowing the land using horses and oxen. The chief showed them a coverlet and a shirt of cotton. The coverlet was embroidered at the edges with silk and colored woolen yarn. The shirt was not pleated at the wrist—as were French garments—and the sleeves were embroidered, as were the shoulders, in various colors. These he had obtained from the whites. The two Frenchmen would have obtained some of these garments to carry back to La Vérendrye had they not exhausted their stock in trade in previous transactions.

The chief went on to remark that Spanish women were white and handsome, wearing their hair in a coil and earrings of brilliant stones as well as bracelets and necklaces of a light yellow color. By means of gestures he showed the two French-men how these whites played the harpsichord and bass viol.

The Spanish, it appeared, were often at war with the Gens du Serpent. They marched in columns, the men wearing armor of chain mail. The chief showed them a Spanish bridle, the bit and curb of which were of one piece, and having long branches, all of it being well polished. Saddles and stirrups were the same as those of the French, who were told that the whites used pistols and saddle cloths (blankets).

The Spanish towns, the Frenchmen heard, were near "the great Lake," the water of which rose and fell and was not good to drink. The country in which they lived was one of very high mountains. Near the white people there were also black men who wore beards and wrought iron; it was necessary to pass

them before one could reach the white settlements. There was
no fear of starving along the way, for animals of all kinds were
to be found everywhere, particularly buffalo and deer. Having
thus offered to guide the two Frenchmen to Spanish lands, he
also expressed a desire to return with them to see the country of
the French.

The tribes who came to trade with the Mantannes
remained among them for more than a month. They frequently
visited the villages, the men learned, and whenever they did so
there was great rejoicing on both sides. In the account that has
been preserved—though it is but an extract of the original
record—we catch a glimpse of the expanding intertribal trade
that followed the acquisition of horses from the Spanish. It is
one of the clearest such accounts available, and sheds light not
only upon the history of their neighbors but on that of the
Mantannes as well. A first dim record of the relations between
the Spanish and the native Indians of the Plains is recorded in
this account. Had the ministry at Versailles the wit to read these
accounts with understanding, they might have thanked La
Vérendrye for obtaining information of such value to them. We
know that the commandant was impressed by the importance
of the information his men had obtained, for the extract
mentioned also records that he had given orders to one of his
sons to proceed with four men and an interpreter to the
Mantannes.

It is unlikely that La Vérendrye expected his son to set off
at once in the fall of 1739, but whatever the expectations,
Pierre, the son, did not actually leave for the Missouri River
country until early 1741. More than a year and a half was
therefore to intervene between the two major contacts with the
Mantannes. We know nothing of independent contacts that
may have been made, by La Vérendrye's men or by those of La
Marque or others, during this time.

La Vérendrye himself spent the winter of 1739 and 1740
at Michilimackinac, and in the spring of 1740 he returned to
Montreal for the first time since the summer of 1737. In the
summer of 1740 he again returned as far as Michilimackinac,
but he spent the winter of 1740 and 1741 at his home in the
East—his first such visit there for many years. When he set out

for the West again in the spring of 1741, he was accompanied by Father Claude Coquart, the first Jesuit to take part in the activities of the western command since Aulneau's death five years earlier. It is regrettable that no clerics took part in the first explorations toward the Missouri; had they done so, we should doubtless have more details of the new peoples. But even in 1741 Father Coquart went no farther west with the commandant than Michilimackinac.

Years later Coquart wrote that during the summer of 1741 he had accompanied a young French officer—by whom he probably means one of La Vérendrye's sons—in a search for the western sea. We know that Pierre and another son left Fort La Reine in April of 1741 to go to the villages of the Mantannes, and the claim was made that he descended the great River of the West to a point "not far from two Spanish forts."[3] Unfortunately, nothing is known of the events of this trip, and we have only his word that it took place. In any event, it is unlikely that Coquart was a member of the party of 1741; had he accompanied it, all record of the fact could scarcely have been lost.

In October 1741, La Vérendrye once more returned to Fort La Reine, from which he had been absent for at least two years. The winter was doubtless spent in consultation and planning between the commandant and Pierre, for by now Pierre was filling his father's shoes in his absence. In the fall of 1741, probably, he had built two new trading posts, one on the shores of Lake Winnipegosis and another on Cedar Lake. The first was named Fort Dauphin (the first of this name), and the second was called Fort Bourbon.[4] These posts were reaching ever nearer Hudson Bay and the English, and much light will surely become available when the records of the Hudson's Bay Company for the period are published, for the English surely kept the French under close scrutiny.

During La Vérendrye's visit to Montreal and Quebec Beauharnois had again warned him that he must carry the matter of the discovery of the Sea of the West to a successful conclusion. The governor warned La Vérendrye that if he returned to Montreal once more without having achieved that goal, he would not be allowed to go out again, or his sons in his place.[5] His official letter sounds as though the governor were being harsh with La Vérendrye, as he undoubtedly intended to make it sound. But in private the governor must have been more reasonable with him. Beauharnois could obviously not excuse his subordinate, and he must have reminded the commandant of the ministry's stubborn adherence to the original plan of discovery. Whatever took place in the East, when La Vérendrye returned to Fort La Reine in October 1741, he again began preparations for an expedition to the southwest rather than to the northwest, which must have seemed to him more promising.

For this expedition he chose his sons François and Louis-Joseph, who were to be the first French to penetrate beyond the upper Missouri River. These men, with the two *engagés* who accompanied them, pushed deeper into the northern plains in what is now the United States than any other explorers of New France. They were absent on this journey for more than a year, facing a variety of unknown terrors hundreds of miles from the now familiar country of the Posts of the North.

6
Explorations of 1742–43 beyond the Missouri River: The Chevalier's "Journal"

Our knowledge of the explorations of the two La Vérendrye brothers in 1742 and 1743 is based on documents preserved in Paris. The most important of them is a letter, unfortunately lacking a place or date, from the Chevalier de la Vérendrye to Beauharnois. A translation of this letter follows. Like the account of the journal of 1738 and 1739, the letter is headed "Journal."

The document is preserved in a draft now in the Archives de la Service Hydrographique. It was first published by Margry, who used it in 1852 in preparing his account of the La Vérendrye family. It is not, however, clear whether the draft now in the Service Hydrographique is the one he published in 1886.[1] Since the published text covers the period from April 29, 1742, to July 2, 1743, it is probable that there actually are (or were) two drafts. Without handling both it would be impossible to determine which text is to be preferred. Probably neither of them, in any case, is the autograph copy of the Chevalier; the original letter was doubtless copied in Quebec for transmittal to Paris.

The translation is based on the published texts of Margry and Burpee, both, presumably, from the same original draft. Other translations have also been consulted.[2] Like that of the letter journal of 1738 and 1739, the text is rendered literally and divided into paragraphs in keeping with custom.

Journal of the expedition [April 29, 1742–July 2, 1743], of the Chevalier de la Vérendrye and one of his brothers to reach the Sea of the West, addressed to M. the Marquis de Beauharnois.

Monsieur,

I take the liberty of submitting to you an account of the journey I made with one of my brothers and two Frenchmen, sent by my father, honored with your orders to proceed to the discovery of the Sea of the West, by way of the Mantanes, following information from the Indians.

We left Fort La Reine on April 29 [1742] and arrived among the Mantanes on May 19. We remained there until July 23, awaiting the Gens des Chevaux [Horse People], whom we were led to expect daily. Seeing that the season was advancing, and being determined not to relax our efforts, I sought among the Mantanes for two men to guide us to the country of the Gens des Chevaux, in the hope of finding some village near the mountain *(la montagne)* or along our way. Two very willingly offered. We did not hesitate a moment to leave. We traveled twenty days west-southwest, which did not promise well for our route. We encountered no one, but plenty of wild animals.

In several places I noticed earths of different colors, such as blue, a kind of vermilion, grass green, glossy black, chalk white, and others the color of ocher. Had I foreseen at the time that I should not go through these regions again, I would have taken some of each kind. I could not burden myself, knowing that I had a very long way to travel.

On August 11 we reached the mountain of the Gens des Chevaux. Our guide did not wish to go farther, and we set to work to build a small house in which to await the first Indians we might discover; we also lit fires on all sides as signals to attract people to us, being resolved to entrust ourselves to the first nations that should appear.

On September 10 only one Mantane remained with us; his

comrade had left to return home ten days previously. Every day I myself went, or sent someone, to the heights to look out. On September 14, our scouts perceived a smoke south-southwest of us.

I sent a Frenchman with our Mantane, and they found a village of the Beaux Hommes [Handsome People], who received them well. By signs, they made them understand that there were three more Frenchmen of us, established *(bâtis)* nearby. The chiefs the next day sent some of their young men with our two men to search for us. We reached the village on the eighteenth and were received with great demonstrations of joy.

Our Mantane asked to be allowed to leave, being fearful of a nation that was hostile to his own. I paid him liberally and gave him whatever was useful and necessary for him to reach home, as I had previously done for his comrade.

We remained with the Beaux Hommes twenty-one days. I did my best to make them understand that they should guide us to a village of the Gens des Chevaux. They answered that some of the young men would guide us as far as the first of them we might meet. I gave them a number of presents, with which they seemed highly pleased.

We left there November [October] 9, by which time we were beginning to understand them easily enough for our needs. Our guides led us south-southwest.

On the second day we came upon a village of the nation of the Petits Renards [Little Foxes], who showed great joy at seeing us. After having made some presents, I had our guides tell them that I was seeking the Gens des Chevaux to guide us to the sea. The whole village set out [with us] at once, still keeping to the same route. I now felt sure that we could only find some sea already known. On the second day of our march we came to a very large village of the same nation. They were very friendly. I made them a number of presents, which they considered great curiosities and appeared to appreciate greatly.

They led us to a village of the Pioya [Kioya, or Kiowa?], which we reached on the fifteenth. There we were very well received. After having made some presents I proposed that they take us to some nation that was on the way to the sea. We continued on our way, to the southwest. On the seventeenth we came to a large village of the same nation. I gave them some presents. We all journeyed together until the nineteenth, keeping to the south, in which direction we reached a village of the Gens des Chevaux. They were in great distress. There was nothing but weeping and howling, all their villages having been destroyed by the Gens du Serpent and very few persons having escaped.

This nation of the Serpent is considered very brave. During a raid they are not content with destroying a village, according to the custom of all Indians; they keep up the warfare from spring to fall. They are very numerous, and woe to those who cross their path! They are not friendly with any nation. It is said that in 1741 they completely defeated seventeen villages, killing all the men and the old women, making slaves of the young women, and selling them on the seacoast for horses and certain merchandise.

Among the Gens des Chevaux I inquired whether there was any knowledge of the nation that lived by the sea. They replied that none of their nation had ever been there, the way being blocked by the Gens du Serpent. By making a long detour we could later see certain nations that traded with the white people of the coast. By means of presents, I persuaded the village to set out and take me to the Gens de l'Arc [People of the Bow], the only nation brave enough not to fear the Gens du Serpent. They have even caused the latter to fear them, through the wisdom and good leadership of the chief who is at their head. I was also given reason to hope that they would be able to give me some knowledge of the sea, since they were on friendly terms with certain nations who go there to trade.

Having traveled steadily southwest, we encountered on November 18 a very large village of the Gens de la Belle Rivière [People of the Beautiful River]. They gave us information about the Gens de l'Arc, who were not far away. We went together to the southwest. On the 21st we discovered their village, which appeared to us very large. All the nations of these regions have a great many horses, asses, and mules, which they use to carry their baggage and for riding, both in hunting and in traveling.

When we reached the village the chief led us to his lodge, treating us graciously and courteously, in a manner that seemed unlike the Indians. He had all our baggage put in his lodge, which was very large, and had special care taken of our horses.

Thus far, in all the villages we had passed through, we had been very well received, but it was nothing as compared with the fine behavior of the head chief of the Gens de l'Arc, unlike all the rest, a man not at all covetous, who always took the greatest care of everything that belonged to us.

I attached myself to this chief, who was worthy of all our friendship. In a short time, through the pains he took to teach me, I understood the language well enough to make myself understood as well as to comprehend what he was able to tell me.

I asked him if they knew the white people of the seacoast, and whether they could take us there. He replied: "We know them through what has been told us by prisoners from the Gens du Serpent, among whom we shall arrive shortly. Do not be surprised if you see many villages assembled with us. Word has been sent in all directions for them to join us. You hear war songs every day; this is not without plan. We are going to march in the direction of the great mountains near the sea, to hunt for the Gens du Serpent. Do not be afraid to come with us; you have nothing to fear, and you will be able to look upon the sea for which you are searching."

He continued his speech thus: "The French who are on the seacoast are numerous. They have a large number of slaves, whom they settle on their lands among each nation. These have separate quarters, marry among themselves, and are not oppressed. The result is that they are happy and do not try to run away. They raise a great many horses and other animals, which they use in working their land. They have many chiefs for the soldiers, and also many chiefs for prayer."

He spoke a few words of their language. I recognized that he was speaking Spanish, and what confirmed me in my opinion was the account he gave of the massacre of the Spanish who were going in search of the Missouri [River], a matter I had heard mentioned. All this considerably lessened my eagerness, concerning a sea already known; nevertheless I should very much have liked to go there, had it been feasible.

We continued our march, sometimes south-southwest,

sometimes northwest, our band continually increasing through the addition of various villages of different nations. On January 1, 1743, we found ourselves in sight of the mountains. The number of warriors exceeded two thousand; these with their families made a considerable band. We continued to march over magnificent prairies where wild animals were plentiful. At night there was nothing but songs and shouting, and scarcely anything was done, except that they came to weep upon our heads, to get us to accompany them in the war. I steadily resisted, saying that we were sent to pacify the country, not to stir up things.

The chief of the [Gens de] l'Arc said over and over that he was troubled on our account, not knowing what all the nations would think of our unwillingness to accompany them. Seeing that we were committed to going with them and could only withdraw on returning from the war, he asked us as a favor to accompany him simply as spectators and begged us not to expose ourselves. The Gens de Serpent, he said, were our enemies as well as theirs, and we must surely know that they were friendly with no one.

We deliberated among ourselves about what we should do. We resolved to follow them, seeing that in our situation it was impossible to do anything else. I had, moreover, a strong desire to see the sea from the top of the mountains. I informed the chief of the [Gens de] l'Arc of what we had decided, and he seemed quite content. A great council was then called, to which we were summoned, as was their custom. Long speeches were made on behalf of each nation. The chief of the [Gens de] l'Arc explained them to me. They all turned upon the measures to be taken for the protection of their women and children during their absence, and how best to approach the enemy. They then addressed us, begging us not to abandon them.

I replied to the chief of the [Gens de] l'Arc, who then repeated to all the assembly my reply that the Great Chief of the French wished all his children to live peaceably and had ordered us to induce all the nations to remain at peace, wishing to see all the country calm and peaceful; that, knowing that their hearts were sick, and with good reason, I bowed my head, and we would accompany them, since they so ardently desired it, but only to aid them with our advice in case of necessity. They thanked us heartily and held long ceremonies for us with the calumet.

We continued our search until January 8. On the ninth we left the village, and I left my brother behind to guard our baggage, which was in the lodge of the chief of the [Gens de] l'Arc. Most of the men were on horseback, advancing in good order. Finally, on the twelfth day, we reached the mountains. In general, they are well wooded, with all kinds of trees, and appear to be very high.

Having come near the main part of the village of the Gens du Serpent, our scouts returned to inform us that these people had made their escape with great haste and had abandoned their dwellings *(cabannes)* and a large part of their belongings. This report brought fear to all our people, who were afraid that the enemy had discovered them, were making for their villages, and would get there before they themselves could. The chief of the [Gens de] l'Arc did what he could to persuade them otherwise and to urge them forward, but no one would listen to him. "It is very annoying," he said to me, "to have brought you this far and to be unable to go any farther."

I was much vexed not to be able to climb the mountains as I had hoped to do. We then decided to return. We had come to this place in very orderly fashion, but the return was very different; everyone fled his own way. Our horses, though good, were very tired and had not fed often enough. I went in company with the chief of the [Gens de] l'Arc, and my two Frenchmen followed us. After having gone a considerable distance without looking behind me, I noticed that they were missing. I told the chief of the [Gens de] l'Arc that I could no longer see my Frenchmen. He replied: "I will halt everyone who is with us."

I retraced my steps at a gallop and saw them at the point of an island, letting their horses feed. Having joined them, I saw fifteen men approaching from the woods, covering themselves with their shields *(paré-flêches)* [cf. parflêches, rawhide containers]. One of them was far ahead of the others, and we let them come within half a musket shot. Seeing that they were preparing to attack us, I thought it advisable to fire several shots at them, which made them retreat hastily. This weapon is highly respected among all these nations, which do not have the use of them, and whose shields cannot protect them against a musket ball.

We remained there until night, after which we set out following our notions [of direction] *(selon notre idée)*, in hope of finding our own Indians. The prairies over which we passed are bare and dry, and the trail of the horses does not show. We continued on our way at random, not knowing whether we were on the right track. We finally arrived, among the first to do so, at the village of the Gens de l'Arc on February 9, the second day of our retreat.

The chief of the Gens de l'Arc had hastened off to stop the band that was marching with us, but they were too frightened to dally on ground so near the enemy. He was very uneasy and the next day had a great "surround" made, to intercept us. He continued to have his people search for us, but without success. He finally reached the village five days after we did, more dead than alive from worry over not knowing what had become of us. The first news he received was that we had returned, fortunately just before the bad weather, for on the day after our return fully two feet of snow had fallen, accompanied by frightful weather. His sadness turned to joy; he did not know how to show us enough affection and friendship.

It surprised us to learn that the chief of the [Gens de] l'Arc, with several others, had divided his people so as to surround us, in hope of finding us. Every day some of them arrived at the village, quite downcast and believing we were lost. All the other nations had separated in order to obtain meat more easily. We continued to travel with the Gens de l'Arc until March 1, going east-southeast all the while.

I sent one of our Frenchmen with an Indian to the Gens de la Petite Cerise [People of the Little Cherry, i.e., Chokecherry], having learned that they were nearby. They were gone ten days on the trip and brought us a message inviting us to go and join them.

I revealed our plan to the chief of the [Gens de] l'Arc, who was greatly affected at finding us resolved to leave him. We were no less affected at parting from him, because of the kind treatment he had always shown us. To console him, I promised to come and see him again, on condition that he consent to settle near a small river that I pointed out and build a fort and raise grain there.

He agreed to everything I proposed, and begged that as soon as I had seen my father at Fort La Reine, I would the coming spring again depart to return and join him. To console him, I promised him everything he desired and made him a present of whatever I thought would be useful to him.

Seeing no opportunity to be taken to the Spanish settlements, and having no doubt that my father would be very anxious about us, we decided to make for Fort La Reine and left the Gens de l'Arc with great regret on both sides. We arrived among the Gens de la Petite Cerise on March 15. They were returning from their winter villages (d'hiverenment), and were two days' march from their fort, which is on the bank of the Missouri.

We reached their fort on the nineteenth and were received there with great demonstrations of joy. I applied myself to learning their language and found it quite easy. There was a man among them who had been brought up among the Spanish and spoke their language like his own. I questioned him often, and he told me all that had been reported to me about him, that he had been baptized and had not forgotten his prayers. I asked him if it was easy to go there. He replied that it was a great distance, that the risks were many on account of the nation of the Serpent and that one would need at least twenty days' time to go there on horseback.

I inquired about their trade. He told me that they had wrought iron and did a great trade in buffalo hides and slaves, giving in exchange horses and goods as the Indians desired, but no muskets or ammunition.

He informed me that three days' journey from where we were, there was a Frenchman who had been settled there for several years. I would have gone to find him if our horses had been in condition. I decided to write him, asking that he come to see us, and saying that we would wait for him until the end of March and hoped to leave at the beginning of April to go to the

Mantanes and thence to Fort La Reine, and also that if he could not come he should at least let us have some news of himself.

On an eminence near the fort I deposited a lead tablet bearing the arms and inscription of the king and placed some stones in a pyramid for the general. I told the Indians, who had no knowledge of the lead tablet I had put in the ground, that I was setting up these stones in memory of the fact that we had been in their country. I should greatly have wished to take the latitude at this place, but our astrolabe had from the beginning of our journey been useless, the ring being broken.

Seeing that April had arrived without news of our Frenchman, and being urged by the guides that I had hired to take us to the Mantanes, and our horses being in good condition, I prepared to leave and made several presents to the chiefs of the nation, who had always taken care of us and treated us well, and also to some of the most important of our good friends.

I left word with the chiefs that if, by chance, the Frenchman I had written to should come to their fort a short while after our departure, he might come and see us among the Mantanes, since we intended to make some little stay there. I should have been glad to get him away from the Indians. I assured the chief of the nation that I would take very special care of the three young men he was letting us have as guides, and that although the Mantanes were their enemies they would have nothing to fear while they were with us.

We left on April 2, to the great regret of the whole nation. They earnestly begged us to come again and see them.

On the ninth, about noon, we came to a village of twenty-five families of the Gens de la Flêche Collée [People of the Glued Arrow], otherwise called the Sioux of the Prairies. We passed among the women and the baggage and stopped for a very short while. They were quite friendly and showed us the place where they were going to camp. We kept within sight of their village, expecting that some of them would come to see us, and keeping constantly on our guard, but no one came.

The next day we resumed our journey, sometimes north-northeast, and sometimes northwest, till we came to the

Mantanes without meeting anyone. We reached that place on May 18. I sent back our guides after having fully satisfied them.

We had intended to remain there fifteen or twenty days to rest and put our horses in good condition, but on the twenty-sixth I learned that there were some Assiniboins at Fort La Butte (*au fort de la Butte*), who were about to leave for Fort La Reine. We quickly made ready to profit by this opportunity and to protect ourselves at the same time from enemies. We passed by Fort La Butte the morning of the twenty-seventh, but the Assiniboins had just left. We had not let them know that we wished to go with them. Two Mantanes came forward who wished to go to see my father and learn the way to our fort. We hastened our pace somewhat and caught up with the Assiniboins at their camp. Their were more than a hundred of them, and we continued our way together.

On the thirty-first our scouts discovered thirty Sioux in ambush along our route. We advanced on them in a body. They were greatly surprised to see so many people and retreated in an orderly fashion, from time to time facing about toward those who came too near them. They were well aware of the kind of men they had to deal with, for they considered the Assiniboins to be cowards. As soon as they saw us, however, all mounted on horses, and recognized us for Frenchmen, they fled in great haste, never looking back. We had no one killed, but several were wounded. We do not know what their losses were, except that one man got among ours [and was captured, according to W. D. Le Sueur].

We reached the village near the mountain on June 2. As our horses were tired, we put off traveling and remained at the village until the twentieth. We then took a guide to lead us to Fort La Reine, which we reached on July 2, to the great satisfaction of my father, who was very anxious about us, it having been impossible to get news to him about ourselves since our departure, and to our own great satisfaction at seeing ourselves out of troubles, perils, and dangers.

7
An Interpretation of the Chevalier's "Journal"

THE La Vérendrye brothers, on their return, had more than doubled their father's explorations south and west from Fort La Reine, probing deeply into what is now western North and South Dakota, probably reaching even the foothills of the Big Horn Mountains in northern Wyoming. Like the account of the explorations of 1738 and 1739, the record of their travels is vague and subject to conflicting claims. Also like the account of the earlier expedition, the account translated in the preceding chapter is not the original document that could be desired.

The account was written by François, the Chevalier, and is not an official draft, but more than likely is a copy, made in Quebec, of his original letter to Beauharnois. It is, in any case, the record as it was seen in Paris by the colonial ministry and by geographers of that center of learning.

Apart from its official character, the account of the events of 1742 and 1743 is in many respects less impressive than the record of the earlier expedition. The Chevalier's letter seems to be a reminiscent account, written without recourse to a field record such as that probably available to the father in 1739. That such a field record was kept by the Chevalier and his brother on their trip is doubtful; at least it would have been difficult to keep such a record, especially during times such as the headlong flight with the Gens de l'Arc and others from the enemy they had gone so boldly to attack.

Although the Chevalier's letter gives several specific dates as well as intervals of time spent at various places or in travel, such statements as occur could readily have been based on recollection. The error of a month that crept into the draft early in the account may be no more than a copyist's error, and is easily corrected. But elsewhere the confusion sounds suspiciously like faulty recollection.

That nothing is known of the time or place at which the account was written suggests something of its reliability. Had it been composed at Fort La Reine in July of 1743, just after the return of the party, it would of course be more reliable than if it were written the following year. There is, however, no reliable evidence on this point; we know only that it was forwarded to Paris by Beauharnois, with a covering letter, on October 27, 1744. It is probably significant that, in the review of all of his efforts in the West written by the senior La Vérendrye at the same time, the father refers to his son's account as but "a little journal," as though to suggest that it was of no great moment; it is even hinted that the account had just been prepared.[1]

Identifiable errors in the letter, such as the entry of *November* for *October*, are less troublesome than other parts of the account itself. Thus, while the party was trying to obtain guides among the Mantanes who could take them to the Gens des Chevaux, it is said that they hoped to find some Indian village "near the mountain" or along the way. The "mountain" alluded to here is obscure. It seems probable that, by anticipation, the Chevalier was referring to the "mountain of the Gens des Chevaux," which he reached twenty days later; but there is no means by which this "mountain" can be positively identified. It can refer only to some feature reached twenty days' travel west-southwest from the Mantanes—which is a matter for speculation.

It seems clear that the course of travel, at least from the time the party left the Mantanes, was erratic at best. The direction seems to have been generally to the southwest, if we accept the readings of the narrative. From the village of the Pioyas, reached October 15, the party is said to have "continued to the southwest." Two days later, having been joined by others of that nation, they continued, "keeping to the south." Yet on November 18, when the Gens de la Belle Rivière were met, we read that they had been traveling "steadily southwest." The text seems unreliable, whether because of discrepancies by a copyist, or because of the Chevalier's faulty memory.

One other case is worthy of comment. About November 21, the French, with the mixed party of Indians, reached the Gens de l'Arc. The Chevalier says that after learning something of their language, he was induced to follow these Indians on a raid to be made in the direction of the "great mountains near the sea." But the direction in which the raid was made is far from clear. We read that the march was "sometimes south-southwest, sometimes northwest." Accepting the text at face value, we have no choice but to infer that the march was made according to the needs of the moment. Later, when the Indians became alarmed at the enemy's hostile disposition toward them and fled in all directions, we read that the French tried to return to the village of the Gens de l'Arc by simply following their "notions" of the right direction. None of this sounds as though directions were by the compass, nor do we read of the use of that instrument in the account at any time.

Even more troublesome in using the document is the matter of the identity of the native groups mentioned. Most of the groups are referred to only by the French version of some native name, and their identity is usually hidden or obscure. Lacking other early sources that might provide information on these groups or linguistic or cultural evidence, students have usually been content with speculation unsupported by verifiable data. Few of the names, in fact, are amenable to identification, for our source is scarcely a document permitting precise historical conclusions. Yet such conclusions have been drawn. The following review of the problem is purposely brief, since the importance of the details has sometimes been greatly overrated and more than occasionally misinterpreted.[2]

The Chevalier's party succeeded in finding a village of a people called the Beaux Hommes after having passed a region of many-colored earths and having reached the "mountain" of the Gens de Chevaux. The region of many-colored earths is

Fig. 7. Some of the North Dakota badlands along the Little Missouri
River in Theodore Roosevelt National Memorial Park. (Photograph
by W. R. Wood.)

surely in the western Dakotas, where the badland topography is so colorful (fig. 7). Although no identification of the "mountain" is really possible, a clear candidate is White Butte in southwestern North Dakota. It is 125 airline miles west-southwest of the Mandan villages at the mouth of the Heart River, the correct direction and about the right distance from the villages. Furthermore, it is the highest point in the state— surely an excellent place for the signal fires the Vérendrye brothers were to kindle.

The Chevalier spoke of his difficulty in communicating with the Beaux Hommes and says that it was finally achieved by means of signs. We can therefore be sure that the Beaux Hommes spoke no dialect familiar to the explorers. Some have identified these people as the Crow Indians.[3] The language of the Crows, however, is closely related to that of the Hidatsas, from whom the Crows had separated,[4] and both languages are related to that of the Mandans. All are dialects of Siouan, and since one of the Mantane guides was still with them, we can safely conclude that the Beaux Hommes were not a Siouan-speaking group. Only after having spent twenty days among the Beaux Hommes did the Vérendrye brothers begin to understand the tongue well enough to make their needs known, so it was obviously not an Algonquian one with which they were familiar.

Who then were these "Handsome People"? Perhaps they were a nomadic bank of the Siksikia, or Blackfeet, who also spoke a dialect of Algonquian, although not closely related to the Algonquian languages with which the Vérendrye brothers were familiar. The Siksikias are apparently called the Beaux Hommes by Arthur Dobbs in his 1744 account of the peoples of the area explored by the Hudson's Bay Company. Dobbs's informant, interestingly enough, was one Joseph La France, a mixed-blood *voyageur* who had deserted from La Vérendrye's command in about 1741, after several years of service in the West. On the other hand, James Mooney says that among the several bands of the Arapahoes were the "pleasant men" (Aqathinenas).[5] Although there is no documentary evidence for the Arapahoes in this area until the last decade of the 1700s, they cannot be dismissed as candidates out of hand. In any event, only further research offers any hope of identification of these "Handsome People." Whoever they may have been, it is possible that they were Algonquian speakers. One thing is clear: the Vérendryes' Mantane scout was afraid of them because they were of a nation "hostile to his own."

The Petits Renards and the Gens de Chevaux of the Vérendrye account must be passed over for lack of any kind of data on them. The Pioyas, however, are probably safely identified as the Kiowa Indians, as they were surely in the general area at that time. In any event, the Petits Renards and the Pioyas were friendly toward one another and apparently toward the Gens de Chevaux as well.[6]

According to the Chevalier's account, he reached the Gens de la Belle Rivière on November 18. Doane Robinson identified this "Beautiful River" as the Cheyenne, whose northern fork is today known as the Belle Fourche (Beautiful Fork). The Cheyenne River, he says, was known to the Sioux as the Wakpa Waste (River Beautiful), and although they were latecomers to the region, he felt that they might have adopted the name by which the stream had been known to their predecessors.[7] The Chevalier gave no weight to this group, merely noting them as being in a large village. It is possible they were an Arikara band: the time of year and the location are about correct for the beginning of a winter hunt.

Francis Parkman was of the opinion that the next group the Chevalier noted in his account, the Gens de l'Arc, was "one of the bands of the western Sioux." A more plausible hypothesis is that these "People of the Bow" were the Pawnees, as Robinson believed.[8]

The account of the Spanish given the La Vérendrye brothers by the Gens de l'Arc chief referred to an event in Spanish colonial history that is well documented—the killing of a number of Spaniards "who were going in search of the Missouri." This event was the massacre of a 1720 expedition under Lieutenant Colonel don Pedro de Villazur. A party under his command had gone toward the east from Santa Fe in a reconnaissance of the northeastern frontier of Spanish territory. The party was attacked and routed by the Pawnees—perhaps with the aid of French traders—and only a few members survived.[9] This event was probably widely reported among the plains Indians and in 1742 would still have been fresh in mind, only twenty-two years after the fact.

We now come to the identity of the enemy against whom the raid was made, the people referred to by the Chevalier as the Gens du Serpent. This group can scarcely be any but the Shoshones, or Snake Indians, as Parkman and others have suggested. Furthermore, his identification of the Gens de la Petite Cerise as the Arikaras is also convincing, for they are known from historical and archeological evidence to have lived about that time in what is now central South Dakota.[10]

One final group remains to be identified before leaving the document prepared by the Chevalier. When the Frenchmen left the fortified village of the Gens de la Petite Cerise, which we must now presume was in the vicinity of modern Fort Pierre, to return to the Mandans, they met a group which the Chevalier called the Gens de la Flèche Colée, or "Sioux of the Prairies." This identification is not especially satisfying, for the group was not overtly unfriendly, and the Sioux were almost universally the archenemy of the plains tribes, as they were to so many of the woodland Indians and the French. Only a few days later, between the Missouri and Fort La Reine, we read that the party discovered some Sioux in ambush along the way—an activity more in keeping with their reputation.

George Will was of the opinion that these "Sioux of the Prairies" were not Sioux Indians at all, as the Chevalier believed, but a band of Cheyennes, although it seems unlikely that this Algonquian-speaking group would be confused with a Siouan-speaking one by the Chevalier. This ethnographic problem probably cannot be solved without far more data than are now available, but an identification as "friendly" Sioux strongly hints that they were the Yanktonais, who were in the general area about that time.[11]

The letter of the Chevalier relating his adventures in 1742 and 1743 has been the subject of speculation from the time it was first made known to historians by Margry. In 1852, Margry felt it was reasonable to suppose that the brothers had reached the Rocky Mountains. When he later published the final volume of his *Découvertes et établissements des Français*, he followed the interpretation of the account given by Parkman, whom he cites, believing that the mountains seen by the

Fig. 8. A view of the Big Horn Mountains, in northern Wyoming. (Photograph courtesy of the Wyoming Travel Commission.)

brothers were the Big Horns (fig. 8) in present-day north-central Wyoming.[12]

Margry was also influenced by the interpretation of Edmond Mallet that the brothers had reached the site of present Helena, Montana. Mallet's contribution has not yet been found in print (or in manuscript)—which is perhaps fortunate, given the free rein to imagination found in it. Since the account is illustrative of the uncontrolled speculation offered by so many later writers, it may serve as an example of numerous other such accounts. From the site of Helena, Mallet speculated, they moved south, passing the Musselshell, where they met the Têtes Plates [sic] (Flat Heads), apparently a corruption of Bougainville's *Gens du plat côté.* Here they crossed the Yellowstone River, moving to the Wind River Range near Fremont Peak, Wyoming, where they were told by the Gens du Serpent of the Green River, a stream south of the Wind River Range and a tributary of the Colorado River. Needless to say, there is nothing in the Chevalier's letter of such wandering as would have taken the brothers that far to the west.

Francis Parkman's contribution to our knowledge of the La Vérendrye brothers was probably written in consultation with Margry, his agent in the Paris archives. His work first appeared in an article entitled "The Discovery of the Rocky Mountains." That the brothers had discovered the Rockies seems not to have been seriously doubted and was accepted by a number of scholars. Parkman himself was cautious in expressing himself and suggested no more than that the brothers, from a distance, probably had a view of the Big Horn Mountains.[13]

The discovery at Fort Pierre, South Dakota, in 1913 of a lead tablet, apparently the one deposited by the La Vérendrye brothers in 1743 and referred to by the Chevalier in his letter, led to much new speculation concerning the route taken during the journey. The reopening of the whole matter of the accomplishments of the family often led to profitless debate between historians. Their arguments, so often based on inadequate evidence and erroneous assumptions, did, of course, bring a certain benefit to history in that they awakened many persons to the more dramatic elements of early western ex-

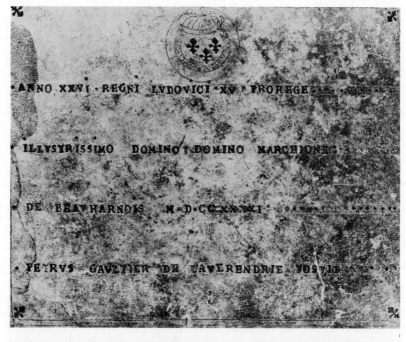

Fig. 9. The lead plate found in 1913 on "Vérendrye Hill" at Fort Pierre, South Dakota. (Photographs courtesy of the Robinson Museum, Pierre, South Dakota.)

plorations. But some of these new interpretations were so riddled with error and so confusing that there is little point in reviewing them in detail. Charles E. DeLand, for example, in a review in 1914 published more than two hundred pages of uncritical speculation on the single subject of the journey of 1742 and 1743.[14]

The circumstances surrounding the discovery of the lead tablet were carefully investigated by Doane Robinson, then superintendent of the South Dakota State Historical Society. This plate, six by eight inches and one-eighth inch thick, was discovered on a hill near the high school building in Fort Pierre on February 16, 1913 (fig. 9). It is now in the collections of the Robinson Museum in Pierre.[15] The obverse carries a die-stamped Latin inscription with the arms of Louis XV; each corner bears a fleur-de-lis. The reverse side bears a brief legend incised in French. The tablet gives every indication of authenticity. It is precisely of the kind that would be expected and coincides with the extant record of the journey of the La Vérendrye brothers. It is in fact strikingly similar to other lead tablets originally deposited by the French as evidence of *prise de possession*. The most important of these are the several lead tablets found in the Ohio River region which were originally buried by the military expedition under the command of Celoron de Bienville.[16]

The text of the French inscription on the plate found at Fort Pierre is one derived after consultation with the Canadian historian Benjamin Sulte and the former French ambassador and scholar Jules Jusserand, by Dr. Louise P. Kellogg of the Wisconsin Historical Society and Doane Robinson and others of the South Dakota Historical Society:

Placed by the Chevalier De La Verendrye Lo [Louis] Jost [Joseph] Verendrye, Louis La Londette and A. Miotte, The 30 March 1743[17]

The tablet reveals, in addition to the names of the two La Vérendrye brothers, the names of the two *engagés* who accompanied them. The names of *engagés* are not often recorded.

The discovery of the tablet, Robinson felt, settled a long-disputed question and definitely fixed the point at which the La

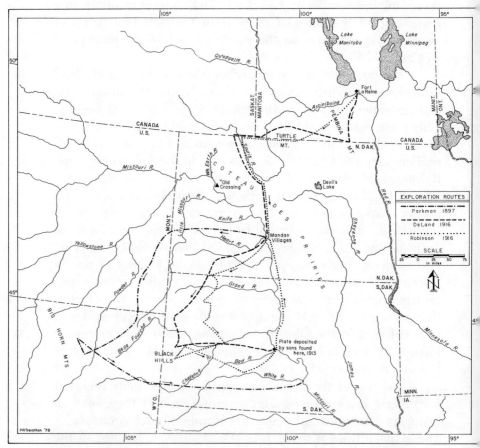

Fig. 10. The routes conjectured to have been taken by La Vérendrye and his sons into the northern plains.

Vérendryes reached the Missouri River on their return—certainly a reasonable contention. He also thought the discovery threw new light on the extent of their explorations. Although he believed that the exact route of the party "must always be a matter of conjecture," certain conclusions were justified.[18]

Robinson (unlike Parkman) was of the opinion that the rate of travel of the party was probably quite slow, so that it was not likely they could have reached the Rockies or the Big Horns in the time available. He concluded that they probably went no farther than the Little Missouri River before turning in a more southerly direction, and that they probably never went beyond the boundaries of the present states of North and South Dakota.[19] His position, that is, was a cautious one, for there is the possibility that the Chevalier's party was on horseback for at least part of the time and could have moved much faster than Robinson believed.

Some of the objections offered in response to Robinson's generally cautious studies are in striking contrast to them. Some studies, in fact, are beneath serious notice.[20] One such statement will serve as an example: that the lead plate could not have been found where it was originally placed in the ground in 1743, so the Fort Pierre area is irrelevant to an understanding of the explorations of 1742 and 1743. Robinson's pungent response to this objection seems to have been generally accepted by most of those concerned with the matter: "To suggest that this plate might have been planted at a distant point, recovered by the Indians and carried to the mouth of the Bad River [at Fort Pierre], there to be fortuitously dropped upon this eminence ["Vérendrye Hill"], precisely complying with the conditions of the record, is a refinement of criticism approaching absurdity."[21]

In sum, the chances seem very good that the La Vérendrye brothers reached a point near the foothills of the Big Horn Mountains, although the Black Hills cannot be rejected out of hand. In any case, the lead plate found near Fort Pierre clearly and precisely identifies one of the major landmarks of their travels, the exact route of which will probably forever remain a matter for speculation.

8
Dénouement

THE explorations of the La Vérendrye brothers and the two
engagés in the lands west of the Missouri River, while in-
teresting as an episode in the history of the exploration of North
America, must have been a major disappointment to them and
to their colleagues. "From the point of view of the Search for
the Western Sea it was nothing but a fiasco. To the Minister
Maurepas it was without significance."[1] The minister's censure
foreshadowed the resignation or recall of La Vérendrye as
commandant of the western posts. He was replaced in 1744 by
a new commandant, Nicholas-Joseph F. de Noyelles. Beauharnois, in a better position to appreciate the facts of the case, had
earlier recommended La Vérendrye for a captaincy, and his
name heads a list of candidates for promotion.[2]

In 1744, La Vérendrye wrote directly to the Comte de
Maurepas, describing his efforts in search of the long-sought sea
and declaring that "the glory of the King and the advantage of
the Colony" had been his sole motives in pursuing this objective.[3] He had, he said, always been eager for the search, but
that he had been the victim of a series of misfortunes, which he
reviewed. Personal profit, however, had never been a primary
consideration, for he was deeply in debt for his efforts. But this
defense of his actions was in vain, for it was made to an ad-

ministrator who consistently showed not the faintest interest in the political expansion or commercial welfare of the colony under his direction. Belatedly, the rank of captain was given La Vérendrye, but he was removed from his former command.

After less than two years in command of the Posts of the West, his successor gave up the struggle. La Vérendrye was again placed in charge of the western division, as if in recognition that he alone was capable of the task. But his own work in the West was at an end, and he did not again leave the settlements. His former champion, Beauharnois—now himself in disgrace—was succeeded by other governors, who, if less able, at least admitted the justice of La Vérendrye's position and defended him as Beauharnois had done. On the very eve of his death, La Vérendrye, whose real merit had gone so long unrecognized, was awarded the Cross of Saint Louis, an honor coveted by colonials like himself.

This is not the place to follow the fortunes of the three sons who survived their father's death on December 6, 1749, although their story and those of the various feeble successors of their father in the West are important to the history of western Canada.

Rather, this is the place to summarize the significance of the explorations of the La Vérendryes into the Missouri River basin in the northern plains of what is now the north-central United States. The experiences of the family in this direction probably offered scant hope of profitable trade, particularly given the problems of transporting the goods to market. That is surely one of the reasons the upper Missouri was less appealing than other areas, such as the Saskatchewan basin, to which La Vérendrye and his successors soon turned.

Yet the struggles of the La Vérendryes had first shown the true character of the geography of this midcontinental region and of its native peoples. If their work bore little fruit, it was not for lack of effort. "It is a great pity," says John B. Brebner "that a natural interest in whether the La Vérendrye group did or did not reach the Rocky Mountains in their journeyings has tended in the past to obscure the importance of their having placed the Missouri and the great rivers of the North-West in their proper relation." La Vérendrye's great work was "to discover and describe the important relation of the three lakes, Winnipeg, Winnipegosis, and Manitoba, to the long rivers which came from the south and west and flowed into Hudson Bay, thereby providing important avenues for the further evaluation of the continent."[4]

More than thirty years were to intervene before the first beginnings of systematic trade in the upper Missouri commenced. When trade was resumed, it followed old French trails. A disastrous war intervened—disastrous at least to the hopes of a French empire in the New World—a war which was to change the destiny of nations. The death of New France marked the birth of modern Canada, and the distant upper Missouri was all but forgotten.

Probably no more thoughtful and understanding appreciation of La Vérendrye and his efforts has been made than that of Arthur S. Morton. He remarks that, "as the King's officer in command of the Postes du Nord," La Vérendrye "had the eye to see the true line of advance for the French, and the way of prosperity for New France. It was to occupy the forest belt that lay to the north-west, rich in the richest furs, to confine the English to a barren and unproductive coast." This action would "pre-empt a continent" for his king. His initial mistake lay "in cloaking this issue by holding out the prospect of an advance to the Western Sea." But La Vérendrye adhered to his vision of the future of his native colony in spite of pressure from those in high places who forced him into vague and unproductive explorations. "When he entered the Upper Country, the English had long won the Indians . . . to their cause and service." But when he died, many of them had been won back to the French."[5]

"Champlain made the East and La Vérendrye grasped the West for the French. Together, they made the French masters of little short of a continent—of a vast domain which smaller men were to lose."[6] In a land in which so many officials were greedy and corrupt, La Vérendrye, "the peer of Champlain in unselfish devotion," cast himself, the lives of his sons, the profits of the fur trade, and even his private fortunes into the scale, and turned the balance in favor of France. The conquest of Canada and the occupation of its West by the British have cloaked his achievements, leaving only geographers and local historians to honor his name. Had he been permitted to follow his plan, says Morton, "he might well have brought the French to the Rockies by way of the River Saskatchewan, the only easy route, within his lifetime, and the honour of his country would not have been tarnished by his death in comparative poverty, a misunderstood and even a maligned man."[7] With this background, we can now better appreciate the acomplishments of the first white man to visit the Mandans in their villages on the upper Missouri River, and those of his sons, who must surely have been the first Europeans to see the Rocky Mountains, and place him and his family among that cadre of explorers which includes also Lewis and Clark.

Notes

Editor's Preface

1. Thomas A. Sullivan, *Proclamations and Orders Relating to the National Park Service*, p. 312; Orin G. Libby to the Commissioner of the General Land Office, August 16 and September 14, 1916, 12–1 Part 1 General, Vérendrye National Monument, Central Files 1907–39, Records of the National Park Service, Record Group 79, National Archives and Records Service, Washington, D.C. The establishing proclamation gave the following legal description of the lands within the boundaries of Vérendrye National Monument: the southeast quarter; the southeast quarter of the northwest quarter; and lots 4 and 5 of Section 14, Township 152 North, Range 93 West of the 5th Principal Meridian.

2. Hillory A. Tolson, comp., *Laws Relating to the National Park Service*, p. 458.

3. Because of the passage of time, subsequent reorganization of the National Park Service, and the death of the author, information on the circumstances of G. Hubert Smith's La Vérendrye research was difficult to gather. Contemporary correspondence relating to both Smith's research and the disestablishment of Vérendrye National Monument is on file at Theodore Roosevelt National Memorial Park, North Dakota, and in the office of the Chief Historian, National Park Service, Washington, D.C. Copies of Smith's original study can be found in both of those places, as well as in the libraries of the Midwest and Rocky Mountain Regional Offices (Omaha, Nebraska, and Denver, Colorado, respectively). Several individuals, including Merrill J. Mattes, Bill Herr, Barry Macintosh, and Frank B. Sarles of the National Park Service; Frank Vyzralek and James E. Sperry of the State Historical Society of

North Dakota; and Alan R. Woolworth of the Minnesota Historical Society, provided information or otherwise furnished assistance to Thomas D. Thiessen, who compiled the historical background for this preface.

Chapter 1

1. Arthur S. Morton, *A History of the Canadian West to 1870–71*, p. 167.

2. Beauharnois to the Minister, September 28, 1733, Archives Service Hydrographiques, Paris (hereafter cited as ASH), 115–11: No. 9, translated in Lawrence J. Burpee, *The Search for the Western Sea*, p. 104.

3. Nellis M. Crouse, *In Quest of the Western Ocean*; Jean Delanglez, "A Mirage: The Sea of the West."

4. Grace Lee Nute, *Caesars of the Wilderness*, p. 34.

5. Carl I. Wheat, *Mapping the Transmississippi West, 1540–1861*, 1:141 and map 131.

6. Morton, *Canadian West*, p. 163; and Abraham P. Nasatir, *Before Lewis and Clark*, Vol. 1, pp. 33n, 62.

7. Morton, *Canadian West*, p. 165.

8. Charlevoix, *mémoire* sent to the Compte de Toulouse, Paris, January 20, 1723, Correspondence, Archives Nationales, Paris (hereafter cited as AC), C11e, 16:102, transcript in the Public Archives of Canada, Ottawa.

9. Beauharnois to the Minister, Quebec, October 1, 1731, AC, C11, 54:385, translated in Burpee, *Search for the Western Sea*, p. 85n, extract.

10. Morton, *Canadian West*, p. 166.

11. Ibid., pp. 166–67.

12. Alanson Skinner, "Notes on the Eastern Cree and Northern Saulteaux," p. 117; David G. Mandelbaum, "The Plains Cree."

13. Nasatir, *Before Lewis and Clark*.

14. Marc Villiers du Terrage, *La Découverte du Missouri et l'histoire du Fort l'Orléans*.

15. Ibid., p. 45.

16. Nasatir, *Before Lewis and Clark*.

17. Mildred Mott Wedel, "Claude-Charles Dutisne."

18. Villiers du Terrage, *La Découverte du Missouri*, p. 126.

Chapter 2

1. Nute, *Caesars of the Wilderness*, p. 15.

2. Harold A. Innis, *The Fur Trade in Canada*, p. 123.

3. Pierre-Georges Roy, *Rapport de l'Archiviste de la Province de Québec pour 1921–1922*, facsimile opposite p. 78.

4. La Vérendrye to the Minister, October 31, 1744, AC, C11e, 16:280–90, published in Pierre Margry, ed., *Découvertes et établissements*

des Français, 6:583–84, and translated in Lawrence J. Burpee, ed., *Journals and Letters of Pierre Gaultier de Varennes de la Vérendrye and His Sons*, pp. 432–35.

5. Morton, *Canadian West*, p. 168; Roy, *Rapport de l'Archiviste . . . pour 1921–1922*, facsimile opposite p. 88.

6. Morton, *Canadian West*, p. 168.

7. Auguste H. Trémaudan, "Who was the Chevalier de La Vérendrye?" Some have felt the Chevalier was Pierre, the eldest surviving son. It is now generally agreed that he was, instead, François, especially in view of the evidence provided by the lead tablet found at Fort Pierre (see Chapter 7).

8. Beauharnois to the Minister, Quebec, September 1, 1729, AC, C11, 51:135, translated in Reuben Gold Thwaites, "Bougainville, Memoir (1757)," p. 167.

9. Coquart to [Father Castel], Quebec, October 15, 1750. Bibliothèque Nationale, Paris (hereafter cited as BN), Manuscrits Français, n.a., 9286: 240, calendared in Nancy M. Miller Surry, ed., "Calendar of Manuscripts in Paris Archives and Libraries."

10. Arthur E. Jones, trans., *The Aulneau Collection, 1734–1745*; Pierre-Georges Roy, "Papers Relating to Aulneau."

11. Morton, *Canadian West*, pp. 168–69, citing Hudson's Bay Company records.

12. De Noyon, *mémoire*, 1750, AC, C11, 52:288, cited in Morton, *Canadian West*, p. 169.

13. Copy in AC, Clle, 16:131, calendared in Surry, "Calendar of Manuscripts."

14. Gonor to Beauharnois, November 3, 1728, ASH, 5: No. 20; BN, Mss., FR., n.a., 2550:123 [Margry copy], calendared in Surry, "Calendar of Manuscripts."

15. La Vérendrye, *mémoire*, [Quebec?], October 10, 1730, AC, F3, 11:304, translated in Burpee, *Journals and Letters*, pp. 43–63.

16. Ibid.

17. [Map of North America, 1730?], BN, Estampes: V^d 22; a copy is in the Karpinski photostats, Newberry Library, Chicago.

18. Charlevoix to the Minister, May 1731, ASH, 115–11: No. 9, copy, translated in Burpee, *Journals and Letters*, pp. 73–81.

19. Morton, *Canadian West*, p. 172.

20. La Vérendrye to Maurepas, Michilimackinac, August 1, 1731, AC, Clle, 16:134; translated in Burpee, *Journals and Letters*, pp. 70–72. Morton, *Canadian West*, p. 172.

21. Louis A. Prud'homme, "Pierre Gaultier de Varennes, Sieur de la Vérendrye"; Morton, *Canadian West*, p. 174; Grace Lee Nute, *Rainy River Country*, p. 7.

22. La Vérendrye to Beauharnois, Fort St. Charles, May 25, 1733, AC, Clle, 16:151: ASH, 115–11: No. 9, extract, translated in Burpee, *Journals and Letters*, pp. 100–102.

23. "Carte d'une partie du Lac Superieur . . . [1733 ?]," BSH, B4044, No. 85, in color, Karpinski photostats. Tracings or drawings derived from this map, both inaccurate and both misleading, are in A. G. Morice, *History of the Catholic Church in Western Canada*, 1:44, and Burpee, *Journals and Letters*, pl. VII, opposite p. 488. Map 2 in Orin G. Libby's introduction to "The Journal of La Vérendrye," opposite p. 234, is derived from part of the drawing in Burpee's *Journals and Letters* and obscures the matter still further.

24. Morton, *Canadian West*, p. 177.

25. Ibid., p. 179.

26. Beauharnois to the Minister, Quebec, September 28, 1733, ASH, 115–11: No. 9; BN, Mss. Fr., n.a., 2552:73, extract, translated in Burpee, *Journals and Letters*, pp. 102–10. A variety of spellings of the term *Ouachipouennes* were used by La Vérendrye. In the passages following, the particular spelling he used at the time in question will be used.

27. La Vérendrye, *mémoire* in the form of a journal of events at Fort St. Charles, May 27, 1733–July 12, 1734, Archives des Affaires Etrangères, Mémoires et documents, Amérique, Paris, 8:46: AC, Clle, 16:173, extract, translated in Burpee, *Journals and Letters*, pp. 133–92. Much the same information appears in a letter of July 23, 1735, from La Jémeraye to Beauharnois, ASH, 115–11: No. 9, copy, translated in Burpee, *Journals and Letters*, pp. 199–201. Since La Jémeraye's statements were derived from La Vérendrye's interviews with the Assiniboins during La Jémeraye's absence, the latter document is not primary evidence.

28. This interpretation was suggested to the editor by Elizabeth P. Henning in a letter of January 24, 1979; she further commented that there are many features in the account which suggest that these westerners were not Indians: they were unlike the Assiniboins or the Crees; the houses had flat roofs covered with earth and *stone*; the dress, except for the material, describes Spanish clothing; the women did not work hard (clearly at variance with plains Indian practice!); and the presence of peas, oats, goats, and domestic fowl, furthermore, do not agree with the customs of the plains village tribes.

29. Francis Parkman, *A Half-Century of Conflict*; Morton, *Canadian West*; Theodore E. Blegen, "Fort St. Charles and the Northwest Angle"; and others.

30. Morton, *Canadian West*, p. 182.

31. Ibid., p. 181n.

32. Ibid., p. 182; Nellis M. Crouse, "The Location of Fort Maurepas."

33. Beauharnois to Maurepas, [after July, 1734), accompanying La Vérendrye's *mémoire*, 1734–35, not separately calendared in Surry, "Calendar of Manuscripts," translated in Burpee, *Journals and Letters*, pp. 117–33.

34. Father Luc François Nau to Father Bonin, Sault St. Louis, October 2, 1735, translated in Jones, *Aulneau Collection*, p. 66.

35. Beauharnois to Maurepas, Quebec, October 8, 1734, AC Clle, 16:[166?], not separately calendared in Surry, "Calendar of Manuscripts," translated in Burpee, *Journals and Letters*, pp. 110–16.

36. Beauharnois to Maurepas, Quebec, October 8, 1734, AC, Clle, 16:169; ASH, 115–11: No. 9, extract, translated in Burpee, *Journals and Letters*, pp. 202–6.

37. Ibid.; La Vérendrye to the Minister, Quebec, October 12, 1734, AC, Clle, 16:166, translated in Burpee, *Journals and Letters*, pp. 193–95.

38. Jones, *Aulneau Collection*; Roy, "Papers Relating to Aulneau."

39. In a letter of April 30, 1736, published in Reuben Gold Thwaites, ed., *Jesuit Relations and Allied Documents*, 68:293, Aulneau says that the Assiniboins traded for corn with the "Kaotiouak or Autelsipounes." In this letter, Aulneau mentions a long conversation he had had with La Vérendrye, who was obviously the source for his information. Aulneau made other references to the Mandans by these names in April 1735, ibid., pp. 236–37, 248–51.

40. Aulneau to Father Faye, Quebec, April 25, 1735, in Roy, "Papers Relating to Aulneau," translated in Jones, *Aulneau Collection*, p. 33.

41. Aulneau to Father Bonin, Quebec, April 29, 1735, in Roy, "Papers Relating to Aulneau," translated in Jones, *Aulneau Collection*, p. 48. Kino's great map first appeared in 1705, in the famous Jesuit *Lettres édifiantes et curieuses* and elsewhere; see Herbert E. Bolton, ed. and trans., *Kino's Historical Memoir of Pimeria Alta . . . 1683–1711*, 1:18. The map appearing in the order's *Memoires de Trevoux* for 1705 is reproduced in Bolton, *Historical Memoir*, vol. 1, frontispiece; see also Wheat, *Transmississippi West*, 1:75–76, 203.

42. La Vérendrye, *mémoire*, October 31, 1744, AC, Clle, 16:282; ASH, 5: No. 17, translated in Burpee, *Journals and Letters*, pp. 435–55.

43. La Vérendrye to Beauharnois, *mémoire* in the form of a journal, June 2, 1736–August 3, 1737, AC, F3, 12:248; ASH, 115–11: No. 9, translated in Burpee, *Journals and Letters*, pp. 213–62; Morton, *Canadian West*, p. 185.

44. Morton, *Canadian West*, pp. 185–86.

45. *Découverte historique: Le Fort St.-Charles retrouvé*; J. Paquin, "The Discovery of the Relics of the Reverend Jean Pierre Aulneau, S. J.,"; Prud'homme, "Pierre Gaultier de Varennes." The skeletal remains were excavated in 1908 by a party of Jesuits from the College of St. Boniface, Manitoba, and were taken to the college with other objects found there. They were destroyed by a fire at the college in 1921.

46. La Vérendrye, *mémoire*, June 2, 1736–August 3, 1737.

47. Ibid.; map, ASH, 4044B, No. 39, photostat in Public Archives of Canada, not in the Karpinski photostats. Tracings have been published in various places: Newton H. Winchell, "The Geology of Minnesota," pl. 3; Gabriel Marcel, *Reproduction de cartes et de globes*, vol. 1, no. 37; Burpee,

Journals and Letters, pl. III, opposite p. 116; and elsewhere, with the statement—apparently correct, but not appearing on the original—"joint à la lettre de M. de Beauharnois du 14 8bre 1737."

48. Burpee, *Journals and Letters*, p. 249n, citing J. B. Tyrrell; Bougainville in Pierre Margry, ed., *Relations et mémoires inédite pour servir à l'histoire de la France dans les pays outre-mer*, p. 187, gives the name in slightly different form: *Jatihilinine.*

49. La Vérendrye, *mémoire*, June 2, 1736–August 3, 1737.

50. La Vérendrye to the Minister, Quebec, October 1, 1737, AC, Clle, 16:192; ASH, 115–11: No. 9, translated in Burpee, *Journals and Letters*, pp. 266–69.

51. Beauharnois to the Minister, Quebec, October 14, 1737, AC, C11, 67:168, translated in Burpee, *Journals and Letters*, pp. 271–73, extract.

Chapter 3

1. Douglas Brymner, trans. and ed., "Journal of La Vérendrye, 1738–39"; Le Sueur in Burpee, *Journals and Letters*; Henry E. Haxo, trans., "The Journal of La Vérendrye, 1738–39."

Chapter 4

1. Parkman, *A Half-Century*, p. 17n.

2. Beauharnois to the Minister, Quebec, August 14, 1739, AC Clle, 16:220, translated in Burpee, *Journals and Letters*, p. 363, extract.

3. Beauharnois to the Minister, Quebec, October 6, 1739, AC, Clle, 16:222, translated in Burpee, *Journals and Letters*, pp. 364–65, extract, "accompanying an extract of a 'journal' of La Vérendrye"; for this, see n. 4, below.

4. Extract of a journal of La Vérendrye, no place or date, AC, Clle, 16:229, translated in Burpee, *Journals and Letters*, pp. 366–73.

5. Russell Reid, "Vérendrye's Journey to North Dakota in 1738," p. 117.

6. This trade has been described by John C. Ewers, "The Indian Trade of the Upper Missouri before Lewis and Clark," and by W. Raymond Wood, "Contrastive Features of Native North American Trade Systems."

7. Burpee, in his 1942 review of Haxo's translation of the La Vérendrye journal, shows that the value of the old French league (of 2.42 miles), which he earlier used in his *Journals and Letters* and which was used by others, may be in error, and that there is good authority for calculating it at 3 English miles.

8. Reid, "Vérendrye's Journey," p. 119.

9. Haxo, "Journal," p. 251.

10. Reid, "Vérendrye's Journey," pp. 118–19.

11. It is so identified in the two articles Warren Upham published in 1906 and 1909 with the same title, "Explorations of Vérendrye and His Sons," and Orin G. Libby, "La Vérendrye's Visit to the Mandans in 1738–39," p. 503.

12. See Libby's 1941 introduction to Haxo's "Journal," p. 232; Reid, "Vérendrye's Journey," p. 118.

13. Chris Vickers, "Archaeology in the Rock and Pelican Lake Area of South Central Manitoba"; idem, "Archaeological Report, 1945"; Katherine H. Capes, "The W. B. Nickerson Survey and Excavations, 1912–15"; E. Leigh Syms, "Cultural Ecology and Ecological Dynamics of the Ceramic Period in Southwestern Manitoba;" idem, "Aboriginal Mounds in Southern Manitoba."

14. Warren Upham, "The Glacial Lake Agassiz," p. 645 and pl. 30; Henry Montgomery, "Calf Mountain in Manitoba." Calf Mountain is in the NE 1/4 of Section 32, Township 2, Range 7 West.

15. Upham, "Lake Agassiz," p. 645.

16. Gordon W. Hewes, "Burial Mounds in the Baldhill Area, North Dakota"; Robert W. Neuman, *The Sonota Complex and Associated Sites on the Northern Great Plains*; Syms, "Aboriginal Mounds."

17. Upham, "Lake Agassiz," p. 41 and pl. 30.

18. Libby, "Visit to the Mandans"; Doane Robinson, "[Map Showing the] Approximate Route of the Vérendrye Brothers, 1742–1743"; idem, "La Vérendrye's Farthest West"; Charles E. DeLand, "The Vérendrye Explorations and Discoveries"; Reid, "Vérendrye's Journey."

19. For example, Libby, "Visit to the Mandans," and others.

20. George F. Will and Herbert J. Spinden, "The Mandans"; George F. Will and George E. Hyde, *Corn among the Indians of the Upper Missouri*; George F. Will, "Criticism of 'Some Vérendrye Enigmas' "; and others.

21. Pierre Margry, ed., "Esquisses de l'Histoire des Colonies Françaises," p. 1410; Parkman, *A Half-Century*; Burpee, *Search for the Western Sea*; idem, *Journals and Letters*; Will and Spinden, "The Mandans"; and others.

22. Libby, "Visit to the Mandans," p. 502. This conclusion is accepted by the French Canadian historian Antoine Champagne, *Les La Vérendrye et le poste de l'ouest*, p. 241, n. 26, in his reevaluation of the original documents relating to the La Vérendrye era. See also Martin Kavanaugh, *La Vérendrye: His Life and Times*, pp. 147–58.

23. Libby, "Visit to the Mandans," p. 503.

24. The French *places* ("open squares"; cf. Spanish *plaza*) was first translated *squares* by Brymner, "Journal." See Alfred W. Bowers, *Mandan Social and Ceremonial Organization*, for details of the ceremonial lodge and for related ceremonies that took place in the plaza.

25. Will, "Criticism," p. 295.

26. Orin G. Libby, "Some Vérendrye Enigmas," p. 144.

27. Roland B. Dixon, review of Libby, "Visit to the Mandans"; Will, "Criticism"; Reid, "Vérendrye's Journey."

28. Will, "Criticism," p. 291; Alice C. Fletcher and Francis La Flesche, *The Omaha Tribe*, p. 102.

29. Libby, "Visit to the Mandans," p. 506; Dixon, review of Libby, "Visit to the Mandans," p. 503; Will, "Criticism," p. 292.

30. Will, "Criticism," p. 291.

31. Ibid., p. 294.

32. Libby, "Vérendrye Enigmas," p. 151.

33. Upham, "Explorations," p. 50; DeLand, "Explorations," p. 167 and map; Robinson, "Approximate Route," p. 90 and map; idem, "Farthest West," map opposite p. 146.

34. Alan R. Woolworth, "Archaeological Investigations at Site 32ME59 (Grandmother's Lodge)"; George Metcalf, "Star Village"; G. Hubert Smith, *Like-a-Fishhook Village and Fort Berthold*.

35. Jon Muller, "Notes on the White Earth Creek Site (32MN2)."

36. Waldo R. Wedel, "Prehistory and the Missouri Valley Development Program," p. 50.

37. Libby, "Visit to the Mandans," pp. 504 n, 505, corrected the error in Brymner's "Journal" concerning these dates.

38. Libby, "Visit to the Mandans," p. 505.

39. Dixon, review of Libby, "Visit to the Mandans," p. 502.

40. Libby, "Vérendrye Enigmas," p. 152.

41. Will, "Criticism," p. 294; Libby, "Vérendrye Enigmas," p. 152 and map facing p. 388.

42. Russell Reid, personal communication to G. Hubert Smith, 1951; idem, "Vérendrye's Journey," p. 126.

43. For example, James Truslow Adams, ed., *Atlas of American History*; Nellis M. Crouse, *La Vérendrye, Fur Trader and Explorer*; John W. Smurr, 'A New La Vérendrye Theory."

44. Walter D. Powell, "Mandan Village Visited by Vérendrye in 1738"; announcements also appeared in the *Minneapolis Journal* for July 19, 1936, and the *Fargo Forum* for December 6, 1936.

45. Thad. C. Hecker, "The Menoken Site" MS, State Historical Society of North Dakota, 1942; Reid, "Vérendrye's Journey," pp. 125–26; George F. Will and Thad. C. Hecker, "Upper Missouri River Valley Aboriginal Culture in North Dakota," pp. 79–80; Kavanaugh, *Life and Times*, p. 152.

46. Hecker, "The Menoken Site"; see also Will and Hecker, "Aboriginal Culture," p. 80.

47. James E. Sperry, personal communication to Ronald Corbyn, 1975, for inclusion in the National Register of Historic Places Inventory Nomination Form for the Menoken Site. On file at the North Dakota State Historic Preservation Office, State Historical Society of North Dakota, Bismarck; and at the National Register of Historic Places, Washington, D.C.

48. Charles E. DeLand, "Aborigines of South Dakota," p. 290; Joseph Henry Taylor, *Frontier and Indian Life and Kaleidoscopic Lives*, p. 303; Will and Hecker, "Aboriginal Culture," p. 81.

Chapter 5

1. Ordinance of Hocquart in the case between de Lorme, plaintiff, and d'Ailleboust, Sieur de Coulonges, defendant [involving La Vérendrye], Montreal, June 12, 1739, AC, Clle 16:240, copy, translated in Burpee, *Journals and Letters*, pp. 515–20. Surry, "Calendar of Manuscripts," errs in giving the date as June 12, 1741.

2. Extract from a journal of La Vérendrye, dated 1740 in pencil, no place, AC, Clle, 16:229, translated in Burpee, *Journals and Letters*, pp. 366–73.

3. Coquart to Father [Castel], Quebec, October 15, 1750, BN, Mss. Fr., n.a., 9286:240, Margry copy, calendared in Surry, "Calendar of Manuscripts," original not known; La Vérendrye to Maurepas, Fort La Reine, May 12, 1742, AC, Clle, 16:253, translated in Burpee, *Journals and Letters*, pp. 377–79.

4. C. L. Wilson, personal communication to G. Hubert Smith, 1951.

5. Beauharnois to the Minister, Quebec, September 25, 1741, AC, Clle, 75:182, transcript in the Public Archives of Canada, not published in Burpee, *Journals and Letters*.

Chapter 6

1. Margry, *Relations et mémoires*, 6:598–611. Parkman, *A Half-Century*, p. 25 n, cites a draft transcribed for him, in preparing his account, "from an original in the Dépôt des Cartes de la Marine"—perhaps that now in the Service Hydrographique—and a duplicate preserved in the Archives des Affaires Etrangères, the latter as that published in Margry. The calendar of the Paris Archives lists only the draft now in the Service Hydrographique, as ASH, 5: No. 18, under the dates April 9, 1742–June 20, 1743, according to Surry, "Calendar of Manuscripts."

2. Margry, *Découvertes*; Burpee, *Journals and Letters*; C. Stanley Stevenson, trans., "The Chevalier de la Vérendrye's 'Journal' "; Anne H. Blegen, ["Journal" of 1742–43]; Le Sueur in Burpee, *Journals and Letters*.

Chapter 7

1. Beauharnois to the Minister, Quebec, October 27, 1744, AC, Clle, 16:277, translated in Stevenson, "The Chevalier," pp. 359–60, and in Burpee, *Journals and Letters*, pp. 402–6; La Vérendrye *mémoire*, annexed to La Vérendrye to Maurepas, no place, October 31, 1744, AC Clle, 16:282, ASH, 5, No. 17, translated in Burpee, *Journals and Letters*, pp. 435–55.

2. Two accounts were discussed briefly at this point in Smith's manuscript: the diary of the Swedish scientist and traveler Pehr (Peter) Kalm, *The America of 1750: Peter Kalm's Travels in North America*, and the memoir of the French naval officer and traveler Louis-Antoine de Bougainville as published in Margry, *Relations et mémoires*. Although Kalm was in Quebec in 1749 and apparently interviewed the elder La Vérendrye, as well as some Jesuits with first-hand familiarity with many of the events he discusses, his account is a hearsay document liberally laced with imaginative and uncritical accounts of the western lands. And although the Bougainville memoir may also be based on sources who had had contact with the senior La Vérendrye, it, too, is based on hearsay information and is very confused. Readers should be aware of these two accounts, as well as the interpretations of the information contained in them—and can judge their merits for themselves. Comments on both accounts were deleted from the text.

3. Parkman, *A Half-Century*, 2:25.

4. W. Raymond Wood and Alan S. Downer, "Notes on the Hidatsa-Crow Schism."

5. Arthur Dobbs, *An Account of the Countries Adjoining Hudson's Bay*, p. 35; James Mooney, "Arapaho," p. 73.

6. Elizabeth P. Henning has suggested to the editor that the Petits Renards may have been the Sand Hills Apaches, for these Apaches and the Kiowas were allied in the late 1700s and the alliance probably had been of some duration. Schlesier, "Rethinking the Dismal River Aspect and the Plains Athapascans," pp. 118–20, fig 4, on the other hand, has identified the Gens de Chevaux as Sand Hills Apaches.

7. Robinson, "Farthest West," p. 149.

8. Parkman, *A Half-Century*, 2:26; Robinson, "Farthest West," p. 149.

9. Gilbert J. Garraghan, "Villazur Expedition."

10. On the identity of the Gens du Serpent, see Parkman, *A Half-Century*, 2:30–31, and Robinson, "Farthest West," pp. 149–50. On that of the Gens de la Petite Cerise, see, for example, Donald J. Lehmer, *Introduction to Middle Missouri Archeology*; and Donald J. Lehmer and David T. Jones, *Arikara Archeology: The Bad River Phase*, for archeological data. There are also elusive ethnographic and linguistic data, as Douglas Parks noted in a letter to the editor dated April 5, 1978:

Melvin R. Gilmore, "Notes on Arikara Tribal Organization," p. 345, listed 12 Arikara bands, each of which had a sacred bundle. Presumably the name of each band and bundle was the same. One of those he listed was *naka:núsč*, which he translated 'Little Cherries'. To date I have been unable to verify this name with contemporary informants. Nevertheless, the name he gave for the Little Cherries is etymologically sound, translating literally as 'little chokecherries'. Given its linguistic soundness and Gilmore's general reliability as a field worker, I feel reasonably confident that there was indeed once such a band or group, even though it is not remembered today. In the 1920s, of course, Gilmore was working with informants who were old men then and were more familiar with the names of old groups or tribal sub-divisions, although they too must have had faulty recollections of tribal subgroupings of a century or more earlier. Indeed, throughout the historic period there has been confusion in band names, since no two recorded lists give exactly the same ones. It is also possible that *naka:núsč* is a village, rather than a band, name. In any case, it undoubtedly designates some Arikara group in the late 18th and/or 19th century.

11. Will and Hyde, *Corn among the Indians,* p. 43 n; Will, "Criticism," p. 297; Elizabeth R. P. Henning, "Plains Ethnohistory and Climate, A.D. 1700–1804," pp. 79–80.

12. Margry, "Esquisses," p. 1410; idem, *Découvertes,* 6:viii–ix (this edition includes a special introduction).

13. Francis Parkman, "The Discovery of the Rocky Mountains." Edward D. Neill, "The First Ioway Indians at Montreal; Visit of First White Men among the Mandans; The Appeal of Chevalier La Vérendrye, the Discoverer of the Rocky Mountains"; Burpee, *Search for the Western Sea;* Upham, "Explorations"; and others. Parkman, *A Half-Century,* 2:29–30.

14. DeLand, "Explorations."

15. Robinson, "Approximate Route," p. 146; "Farthest West."

16. Thwaites, "Bougainville," p. 44.

17. Robinson, "Approximate Route."

18. Robinson, "Farthest West," p. 147.

19. Ibid., p. 148.

20. For example, Libby, "Vérendrye Enigmas."

21. Doane Robinson, reply to Libby, "Some Vérendrye Enigmas," p. 377.

Chapter 8

1. Morton, *Canadian West,* p. 198.

2. Beauharnois to the Minister, Quebec, October 20, 1743, AC, Clle, 79:195, calendared in Surry, "Calendar of Manuscripts," transcript in the Public Archives of Canada.

3. La Vérendrye to the Minister, Quebec, October 31, 1744, AC, Clle, 16:280–90, translated in Stevenson, "The Chevalier," pp. 361–62, and in Burpee, *Journals and Letters,* pp. 432–35. The letter was accompanied by a memoir of the same date, AC, Clle, 16:282; ASH, 5, No. 17, translated in Burpee, *Journals and Letters,* pp. 435–55.

4. John Bartlet Brebner, *The Explorers of North America, 1492–1806,* p. 359.

5. Morton, *Canadian West,* p. 205.

6. Ibid.

7. Ibid., p. 206.

References

Archival Material

NATIONAL ARCHIVES AND RECORDS SERVICE, Washington, D.C.
Record Group 79, Records of the National Park Service, Vérendrye National Monument, Central Files 1907–39.

PUBLIC ARCHIVES OF CANADA, Ottawa
Karpinski photostats of manuscript maps of the French regime, and other maps, both manuscript and published. Copies in the Newberry Library, Chicago.

La Vérendrye, Pierre Gaultier de Varennes, Sieur de. "Journals en form de Letre . . . (1738–39)." Original MS, 22 pp., foolscap. Received from the family of "the late Judge Badgley, Montreal," according to Douglas Brymner, "Journal of La Vérendrye, 1738–39," p. viii. Published in Brymner, "Journal," and Lawrence J. Burpee, ed., *Journals and Letters of . . . la Vérendrye. . . .*

Margry transcripts from the Paris Archives. Numerous documents from the period of La Vérendrye's explorations, still unpublished. Texts are not reliable.

STATE HISTORICAL SOCIETY OF NORTH DAKOTA, Bismarck
Thad. C. Hecker. "White Earth Creek Village Site." MS (1938), 4 pp. plus a map and photographs. A report of excavations at this site in northwest Mountrail County, North Dakota. For a published account of the site, see Jon Muller, "Notes on the White Earth Creek Site (32MN2)."
_____. "The Menoken Site." MS (1942), 6 pp. A report on excavations at the site.

Orin G. Libby Papers. Libby's correspondence as secretary of the State Historical Society, and his research notes on La Vérendrye.

Walter D. Powell. "Vérendrye: Discovery of the Western Mountains in 1742 and 1743." Typescript (1940), 17 pp.

———. "Long-sought Indian Village Located. . . ." Typescript (n.d.), 9 pp.

Published and Other Sources

Adams, James Truslow, ed. *Atlas of American History*. New York: Charles Scribner's Sons, 1946.

Blegen, Anne H., trans. ["Journal of 1742–43."] *Oregon Historical Society Quarterly* 26 (1925): 116–27.

Blegen, Theodore C. "Fort St. Charles and the Northwest Angle." *Minnesota History* 18 (1937): 231–48.

Bolton, Herbert E., ed. and trans. *Kino's Historical Memoir of Pimería Alta . . . 1683–1711.* 2 vols. Cleveland: Arthur H. Clark Co., 1919.

Bowers, Alfred W. *Mandan Social and Ceremonial Organization.* Chicago: University of Chicago Press, 1950.

Brebner, John Bartlet. *The Explorers of North America, 1492–1806.* New York: Macmillan, 1933.

Brymner, Douglas, trans. and ed. "Journal of La Vérendrye, 1738–39." In "Report on Canadian Archives, 1889." Appendix to *Report of Minister of Agriculture*, pp. 1–29. Ottawa, 1890. (French and English texts, both unreliable. English translation reprinted in *Oregon Historical Society Quarterly* 26 (1925): 86–115.

Burpee, Lawrence J. *The Search for the Western Sea: The Story of the Explorations of North-Western America.* Toronto: Musson Book Co., 1908.

———. "La Vérendrye's 1738–39 Journal." [Review of Haxo, "The Journal of La Vérendrye, 1738–39"]. *Canadian Historical Review* 23 (1942): 407–11.

Burpee, Lawrence J., ed. *Journals and Letters of Pierre Gaultier de Varennes de la Vérendrye and His Sons.* Publications of the Champlain Society, vol. 16. Toronto: Ballantyne Press, 1927. (Translations by W. D. Le Sueur. French and English texts. Essential for any study of the La Vérendryes, although the texts are not reliable, being largely from the Margry transcripts.)

Capes, Katherine H. "The W. B. Nickerson Survey and Excavations, 1912–15, of the Southern Manitoba Mounds Region." National Museum of Canada, Ottawa, *Anthropological Papers*, no. 4, 1963.

Catlin, George. *O-kee-pa.* Philadelphia: Lippincott, 1867.

Champagne, Antoine. *Les La Vérendrye et le poste de l'ouest.* Quebec City: Laval University Press, 1968.

Crouse, Nellis M. *In Quest of the Western Ocean.* London: J. Dent and Sons, 1928.

_____. "The Location of Fort Maurepas." *Canadian Historical Review* 9 (1928): 206–22.

_____. *La Vérendrye, Fur Trader and Explorer.* Ithaca, N.Y.: Cornell University Press, 1956.

Découverte historique: Le Fort St.-Charles Retrouvé . . . in Les Cloches de Saint-Boniface (organe de l'Archevêqué et de toute la province ecclésiastique de Saint-Boniface, vol. 7, pp. 205–34, 1908. Reprinted and bound as part of *Bulletin de la Société historique de Saint-Boniface,* vol. 1. Saint-Boniface, Manitoba, 1911.

DeLand, Charles E. "Aborigines of South Dakota, Part II: Mandan." *South Dakota Historical Collections* 4 (1908): 275–730.

_____. "The Vérendrye Explorations and Discoveries, Leading to the Planting of the Fort Pierre Tablet." *South Dakota Historical Collections* 7 (1914): 99–322.

_____. Reply to Libby, "Some Vérendrye Enigmas". In "Additional Vérendrye Material," *Mississippi Valley Historical Review* 3 (1916): 378–86.

Delanglez, Jean. "A Mirage: The Sea of the West." *Revue d'histoire de l'Amérique française* 1 (1947–48): 346–81, 541–68.

Dixon, Roland B. Review of Libby, "La Vérendrye's Visit to the Mandans in 1738–39". *American Anthropologist* 11 (1909): 498–503.

Dobbs, Arthur. *An Account of the Countries Adjoining Hudson's Bay, in the North-West Part of America.* London, 1744.

Ewers, John C. "The Indian Trade of the Upper Missouri before Lewis and Clark: An Interpretation." *Missouri Historical Society Bulletin* 10 (1954): 429–46.

Fletcher, Alice C., and Francis La Flesche. *The Omaha Tribe.* Twenty-seventh Annual Report of the Bureau of American Ethnology. Washington, D.C.: Government Printing Office, 1911.

Garraghan, Gilbert J. "Villazur Expedition." In *Dictionary of American History,* edited by J. T. Adams, 5: 369. New York: Charles Scribner's Sons, 1946.

Gilmore, Melvin R. "Notes on Arikara Tribal Organization." *Indian Notes* (New York: Museum of the American Indian, Heye Foundation) 4 (1927): 332–50.

Haxo, Henry E., trans. "The Journal of La Vérendrye, 1738–39." *North Dakota History* 8 (1941): 229–71.

Henning, Elizabeth R. P. "Plains Ethnohistory and Climate, A.D. 1700–1804." M.A. thesis, University of Nebraska–Lincoln, 1977.

Hewes, Gordon W. "Burial Mounds in the Baldhill Area, North Dakota." *American Antiquity* 14 (1949): 322–28.

Innis, Harold A. *The Fur Trade in Canada: An Introduction to Canadian Economic History.* New Haven, Conn.: Yale University Press, 1930.

Jones, Arthur E., trans. *The Aulneau Collection, 1734–1745.* Montreal, 1893.

Kalm, Pehr (Peter). *The America of 1750: Peter Kalm's Travels in North*

America: The English Version of 1770. Edited, revised, and translated from the original Swedish by Adolph B. Benson. 2 vols. New York: Wilson-Erickson, 1937.

Kavanaugh, Martin. *La Vérendrye: His Life and Times.* 2d ed. Brandon, Manitoba: M. Kavanaugh, 1968.

Lehmer, Donald J. *Introduction to Middle Missouri Archeology.* National Park Service Anthropological Papers, no. 1. Washington, D.C.: Government Printing Office, 1971.

Lehmer, Donald J., and David T. Jones, *Arikara Archeology: The Bad River Phase.* Publications in Salvage Archeology, no. 1. Lincoln, Nebr.: Smithsonian Institution, River Basin Surveys, 1968.

Libby, Orin G. "La Vérendrye's Visit to the Mandans in 1738–39." *State Historical Society of North Dakota Collections* 2 (1908): 502–8.

———. "The Mandans from the Archaeological and Historical Standpoint." *Proceedings of the Mississippi Valley Historical Association for 1907–1908.* Vol. 1 (1909), pp. 56–63.

———. "The Proper Identification of Indian Village Sites in North Dakota: A Reply to Dr. Dixon." *American Anthropologist* 12 (1910): 123–28.

———. "Some Vérendrye Enigmas." *Mississippi Valley Historical Review* 3 (1916): 143–60.

———. Introduction to "The Journal of La Vérendrye, 1738–39," edited by Henry E. Haxo. *North Dakota Historical Quarterly* 8 (1941): 229–41.

Mandelbaum, David G. "The Plains Cree." *American Museum of Natural History Anthropological Papers* 37 (1940): 155–316.

Marcel, Gabriel. *Reproduction de cartes et de globes relatifs à la découverte de l'Amérique du XVI au XVIIIe siècle, avec texte explicatif.* 2 vols. Paris, 1893.

Margry, Pierre, ed. "Esquisses de l'histoire des colonies françaises—Las Varennes de la Vérendrye, d'après les documents inédits tirés des archives des divers départements de l'état." *Moniteur Universel,* no. 258 (September 14, 1852), pp. 1408–10; no. 306 (November 1, 1852), pp. 1773–74.

———. *Relations et mémoires inédite pour servir à l'histoire de la France dans les pays outre-mer, tirés des archives du Ministère de la Marine et des Colonies.* Paris, Challamel aîné, 1867. (Reprinted in Pierre-Georges Roy, *Rapport de l'archiviste de la province de Québec pour 1923–1924*; translated in Reuben Gold Thwaites, "Bougainville, Memoir (1757)," extracts.)

———. *Découvertes et établissements des français dans l'ouest et dans le sud de l'Amérique Septentrionale.* 6 vols. Paris, 1879–86.

Metcalf, George. *Star Village: A Fortified Historic Arikara Site in Mercer County, North Dakota.* Bureau of American Ethnology Bulletin 185, River Basin Surveys Papers, no. 27. Washington, D.C.: Government Printing Office, 1963.

Montgomery, Henry. "Calf Mountain in Manitoba." *American Anthropologist* 12 (1910): 49–57.

Mooney, James. "Arapaho." In *Handbook of American Indians North of Mexico*, edited by F. W. Hodge. vol. 1. Bureau of American Ethnology Bulletin 30. Washington, D.C.: Government Printing Office, 1907.

Morice, A. G. *History of the Catholic Church in Western Canada.* 2 vols. Toronto, Musson Book Co., 1910.

Morton, Arthur S. *A History of the Canadian West to 1870-71.* Toronto, T. Nelson, 1939.

Muller, Jon. "Notes on the White Earth Creek Site (32MN2)" *Plains Anthropologist* 3 (1968): 18-25.

Nasatir, Abraham P. *Before Lewis and Clark.* 2 vols. St. Louis: St. Louis Historical Documents Foundation, 1952.

Neill, Edward D. *Sieur de La Vérendrye and His Sons, the Discoverers of the Rocky Mountains, by Way of Lakes Superior and Winnipeg, and Rivers Assineboin and Missouri. . . .* Minneapolis, 1875. (Reprinted with editorial notes by Granville Stuart in *Contributions to the Historical Society of Montana* 1 (1902): 261 ff; based on Margry, "Esquisses de l'histoire des colonies françaises.")

―――. "The First Ioway Indians at Montreal; Visit of First White Men among the Mandans; The Appeal of Chevalier La Vérendrye, the Discoverer of the Rocky Mountains." In *Macalester College Contributions, Department of History, Literature and Political Science,* 2d ser., no. 5, pp. 109-24. St. Paul, 1892. (The second topic is a summary of the journal of 1738-39, following Brymner, "Journal of La Vérendrye, 1738-39." The third topic is a translation by John H. Ames of Chr. de la Vérendrye to the Minister, Montreal, September 30, 1750. Other translations are in Stevenson, "The Chevalier," and Burpee, *Journals and Letters.*

Neuman, Robert W. *The Sonota Complex and Associated Sites on the Northern Great Plains.* Nebraska State Historical Society Publications in Anthropology, no. 6, 1975.

Nute, Grace Lee. *Caesars of the Wilderness: Medard Chouart, Sieur de Groseilliers and Pierre Esprit Radisson, 1618-1710.* New York: American Historical Association, 1943.

―――. *Rainy River Country: A Brief History of the Region Bordering Minnesota and Ontario.* St. Paul: Minnesota Historical Society, 1950.

Paquin, J. "The Discovery of the Relics of the Reverend Jean Pierre Aulneau, S.J." *Bulletin de la Société historique de Saint-Boniface* 1 (1911): 58-76.

Parkman, Francis. "The Discovery of the Rockey Mountains. *Atlantic Monthly* 61 (1888): 783-93.

―――. *A Half-Century of Conflict.* 2 vols. Boston: Little, Brown and Co., 1897. (A classic account of the La Vérendryes, requiring but minor emendations.)

Paullin, Charles O., and Wright, John K., eds. *Atlas of the Historical Geography of the United States.* Carnegie Institution of Washington Publication no. 401. Washington, D.C.: Carnegie Institution of Washington, 1932.

Powell, Walter D. "Mandan Village Visited by Vérendrye in 1738." *Minnesota Archaeologist* 2 (1936): 4–6.

Prud'homme, Louis A. "Pierre Gaultier de Varennes, Sieur de la Vérendrye, Captain of Marines, Chevalier of the Military Order of St. Louis, Discoverer of the North-West." *Bulletin of the Historical Society of Saint-Boniface* 5, pt. 2 (1916).

Reid, Russell. "Vérendrye's Journey to North Dakota in 1738." *North Dakota History* 32 (1965): 117–29.

Robinson, Doane. "[Map Showing the] Approximate Route of the Vérendrye Brothers, 1742–1743." *South Dakota Historical Collections* 7 (1914): 90.

_____. "La Vérendrye's Farthest West." *Proceedings of the 61st Annual Meeting of the Wisconsin Historical Society, 1913* (1914), pp. 146–50.

_____. "The Vérendrye Plate." *Proceedings of the Mississippi Valley Historical Association for 1913–14*, vol. 7 (1914), pp. 244–53.

_____. Reply to Libby, "Some Vérendrye Enigmas." *Mississippi Valley Historical Review* 3 (1916): 368–77.

Roy, Pierre-Georges. *Rapport de l'archiviste de la province de Québec pour 1921–1922*. Quebec, 1922.

_____. *Rapport de l'archiviste de la province de Québec pour 1923–1924*, pp. 42–70. Quebec, 1924.

_____. "Papers Relating to Aulneau." *Rapport de l'archiviste de la province de Québec pour 1926–1927*, pp. 259–330. Quebec, 1927.

Skinner, Alanson. "Notes on the Eastern Cree and Northern Saulteaux." *American Museum of Natural History Anthropological Papers* 9 (1911): 117–77.

Smith, G. Hubert. *Like-a-Fishhook Village and Fort Berthold, Garrison Reservoir, North Dakota*. National Park Service Anthropological Papers 2. Washington, D.C.: Government Printing Office, 1972.

Smurr, John W. "A New La Vérendrye Theory." *Pacific Northwest Quarterly* 43 (1952): 51–64.

Stevenson, C. Stanley, trans. "The Chevalier de la Vérendrye's 'Journal,' 1742–43, and Other Documents." *South Dakota Historical Collections* 7 (1914): 349–58.

Schlesier, Karl H. "Rethinking the Dismal River Aspect and the Plains Athapascans, A.D. 1692–1768." *Plains Anthropologist* 17 (1972): 101–33.

Sullivan, Thomas A., comp. *Proclamations and Orders Relating to the National Park Service up to January 1, 1945*. Washington, D.C.: Government Printing Office, 1945.

Surry, Nancy M. Miller, ed. *Calendar of Manuscripts in Paris Archives and Libraries Relating to the History of the Mississippi Valley to 1803*. 2 vols. Vol. 1, 1581–1739; vol. 2, 1740–1803. Washington, D.C.: Carnegie Institution of Washington, 1926–28.

Syms, E. Leigh. *Cultural Ecology and Ecological Dynamics of the Ceramic*

Period in Southwestern Manitoba. Plains Anthropologist Memoir 12 (1977).

————. "Aboriginal Mounds in Southern Manitoba: An Evaluative Overview." Research manuscript submitted to Parks Canada, 1978.

Taylor, Joseph Henry. *Frontier and Indian Life and Kaleidoscopic Lives.* Valley City, N.D.: E. P. Gitchell, 1932.

Thwaites, Reuben Gold. *France in America, 1497–1763.* New York: Harper and Brothers, 1905.

Thwaites, Reuben Gold, ed. *Jesuit Relations and Allied Documents.* 73 vols. Cleveland: Burrows Brothers, 1896–1901.

————. *Original Journals of the Lewis and Clark Expedition, 1804–1806.* 8 vols. New York: Dodd, Mead and Co., 1904–1905.

————. "Bougainville, Memoir (1757)." *Wisconsin Historical Society Collections* 18 (1908): 167–95.

Tolson, Hillory A., comp. *Laws Relating to the National Park Service: Supplement II, May 1944 to January 1963.* Washington, D.C.: Government Printing Office, 1963.

Trémaudan, Auguste H. "Who was the Chevalier de La Vérendrye?" *Canadian Historical Review* 1 (1920): 246–54.

Upham, Warren. *The Glacial Lake Agassiz.* U.S. Geological Survey Monograph 25. Washington, D.C.: Government Printing Office, 1895.

————. "Explorations of Vérendrye and His Sons, from Lake Superior to the Rocky Mountains, 1728 to 1749." *Bulletin of the Minnesota Academy of Sciences* 4 (1906): 277–81.

————. "The Explorations of Vérendrye and His Sons." *Proceedings of the Mississippi Valley Historical Association for 1907–08.* vol. 1 (1909), pp. 43–55.

Vickers, Chris. "Archaeology in the Rock and Pelican Lake Area of South Central Manitoba." *American Antiquity* 11 (1945): 88–94.

————. *Archaeological Report, 1945.* Projects of the Historical and Scientific Society of Manitoba, Winnipeg, 1948.

Villiers du Terrage, Marc. *La Découverte du Missouri et l'histoire du Fort l'Orléans (1673–1728).* Paris: H. Champion, 1925.

Wedel, Mildred Mott. "Claude Charles Dutisne: A Review of His 1719 Journey." *Great Plains Journal* 12 (1972–73): 4–25, 146–73.

Wedel, Waldo R. "Prehistory and the Missouri Valley Development Program: Summary Report on the Missouri River Basin Archeological Survey in 1947." *Smithsonian Miscellaneous Collections* 111 (1948): 1–52.

Wheat, Carl I. *Mapping the Transmississippi West, 1540–1861.* Vol. 1. San Francisco: Institute of Historical Cartography, 1957.

Will, George F. "Criticism of 'Some Vérendrye Enigmas.' " *American Anthropologist* 19 (1917): 291–97.

Will, George F., and Hecker, Thad. C. "Upper Missouri River Valley Aboriginal Culture in North Dakota." *North Dakota Historical Quarterly* 11 (1944): 5–126.

Will, George F., and Hyde, George E. *Corn among the Indians of the Upper Missouri*. St. Louis: William H. Miner Co., 1917.

Will, George F., and Spinden, Herbert J. "The Mandans: A Study of their Culture, Archaeology, and Language." *Papers of the Peabody Museum of American Archaeology and Ethnology* 3 (1906): 79–219.

Winchell, Newton H. *The Geology of Minnesota: Volume 1 of the Final Report*. Geological and Natural History Survey of Minnesota. Minneapolis, 1884.

Wood, W. Raymond. "Contrastive Features of Native North American Trade Systems." *University of Oregon Anthropological Papers* 4 (1972): 153–69.

Wood, W. Raymond, and Downer, Alan S. "Notes on the Crow-Hidatsa Schism." *Plains Anthropologist Memoir* 13 (1977): 83–100.

Woolworth, Alan R. "Archaeological Investigations at Site 32ME59 (Grandmother's Lodge)." *North Dakota History* 23 (1956): 79–102.

Index